20

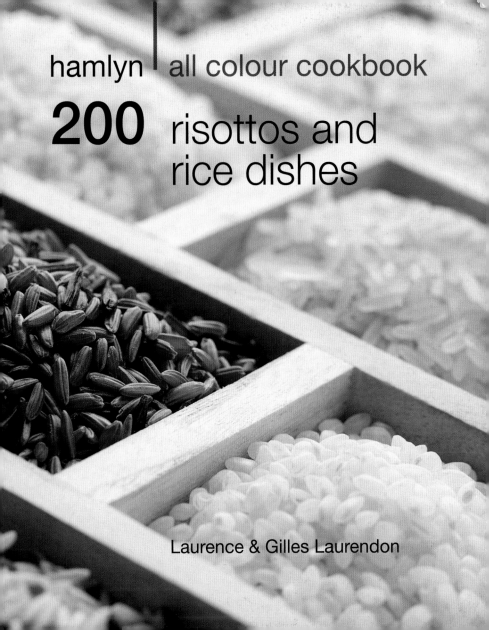

hamlyn | all colour cookbook

200 risottos and rice dishes

Laurence & Gilles Laurendon

An Hachette UK Company
www.hachette.co.uk

First published in Great Britain in 2011 by
Hamlyn a division of Octopus Publishing Group Ltd,
Endeavour House, 189 Shaftesbury Avenue,
London, WC2H 8JY
www.octopusbooks.co.uk

This title was originally published as Riz Gourmond
(copyright © Hachette-Livre Marabout 2004)

ISBN: 978-0-600-62267-3

A CIP catalogue reco...

The Department of Health ...
consumed raw. This book ...
raw or lightly cooked eggs. It ...
such as pregnant and nurs...
babies and young chil...
cooked dishes made with eggs. Once prepared, these dishes
should be kept refrigerated and used promptly.

This book includes dishes made with nuts and nut
derivatives. It is advisable for those with known allergic
reactions to nuts and nut derivatives and those who may be
potentially vulnerable to these allergies to avoid dishes made
with nuts and nut oils. It is also prudent to check the labels of
pre-prepared ingredients for the possible inclusion of
nut derivatives.

Both metric and imperial measurements have been given
in all recipes. Use one set of measurements only, and not a
mixture of both.

Standard level spoon measurements are used in all recipes.
1 tablespoon = one 15 ml spoon
1 teaspoon = one 5 ml spoon

Ovens should be preheated to the specified temperature –
if using a fan-assisted oven, follow the manufacturer's
instructions for adjusting the time and temperature.

Fresh herbs should be used unless otherwise stated.

contents

introduction

introduction

Rice is one of the world's most widely eaten cereals. It is the staple diet of many human populations and an important element in Asian cuisine, notably that of China and India. In Europe it is cultivated in Italy's Po Valley, the Camargue region of France, the Iberian Peninsula, Greece and even in Russia.

rice is simple and good!

It's amazing what you can make with rice. It's the main ingredient of such unique, nourishing dishes as the paella of Spain or the risotto of Italy. You can use it to feed your family in many ways. Serve Cantonese rice or plain white rice with fish or meat dishes. Take a rice salad to a picnic lunch in the park or make sushi for an intimate supper. Rice is also an excellent sweet dish: there's nothing so comforting as a milky rice pudding. It's simple and good.

rice is healthy!

Rice has remarkable nutritional qualities. It contains beneficial vitamins, minerals and fibres.

Because rice is starchy it is an energy source, which gradually releases its complex carbohydrates into the system to provide energy. Rice also contains other useful nutrients such as B-group vitamins, magnesium, vegetable protein, iron and calcium.

Nutritionists recommend rice and, what's more, it isn't fattening.

instant rice

Good quality precooked, steamed or easy-cook rice is now available and it's useful to keep some in your store cupboard. This rice takes 5–10 minutes to prepare and is particularly handy for last-minute cooking. It's perfect for microwaving and can also be cooked on the hob or oven.

what rice to choose?

White rice is generally far more popular than wholegrain (brown) rice, as people tend to prefer its taste and colour. However, white rice is completely lacking in the germ and bran, and the process of dehusking and polishing the rice removes most of its nutrients.

Brown rice is a better nutritional choice. Wholegrains retain their external casing and are rich in vitamins and minerals. The browner the rice, the more complete its nutrients and the more nourishing and tasty it is.

Long-grain rice, such as basmati, Suriname or Thai fragrant rice, does not stick during cooking. These rices are generally used in salads or as a side dish. Short-grain rice such as arborio is suitable for risottos.

types of rice

Yellow, white, black, wholegrain, sticky – there's no need to just confine yourself to long-grain white rice. There are thousands of rice varieties of differing colours, flavours and shapes. This book introduces some of the more popular varieties, all of which are easy to find in shops and supermarkets. There is also an enormous range of products made from rice, such as rice noodles, rice crackers and the delicate pancakes used to wrap spring rolls, not to mention creamed rice, a feature of Middle Eastern cuisine, or the mochi rice paste used in Japan to make amazing cakes. The choice is yours!

9

creole-style rice

This is the most common way of cooking rice, worldwide. It's also the simplest and is suitable for almost all rice varieties.

plenty of water

There are two ways of cooking rice in water. Pour the rice into a large saucepan of boiling water, as with pasta (rice should always 'swim freely'), bring it back to the boil, cook it, uncovered, for the required time, then drain it. Alternatively, add 1 part of rice to 1½ times its volume of hot liquid, then let it simmer, covered, until all the liquid has been absorbed.

flavouring the cooking water

Depending on the recipe, you can use:

- chicken, vegetable or meat stock

- spices: cinnamon, chilli, ginger, nutmeg, clove

- the rind of citrus fruits (orange, lemon)

- or aromatic herbs: thyme, bay, rosemary, chives, parsley, coriander, lemongrass.

creole rice step-by-step

Serves **4**
300 ml (½ pint) **water** or **stock**
180 g (6 oz) **rice**
salt and **pepper**

Bring the water or stock to the boil in a large saucepan. Season with salt and pepper, add the rice and cover.

Return to the boil then lower the heat and cook gently, covered, for 12–15 minutes.

Drain the rice. Set aside and keep warm or serve immediately.

steamed rice

This method of cooking aerates the rice and makes it light and very tender. The rice must first be steeped in cold water for 1 hour then placed in a steamer over boiling water. Allow about 25 minutes cooking time.

what rice is suitable for steaming?

Steaming is particularly appropriate for sticky rice but long or short-grain rice can also be cooked by this method, provided it has been steeped in water for at least an hour beforehand.

steeping

The longer you steep the rice in water, the shorter the cooking time.

rice-cooker

You could also use a rice-cooker, a piece of kitchen equipment specially designed to steam-cook rice. This electric utensil creates perfectly cooked rice, with well-separated grains.

aromatize it

To give a delicate fragrance to steamed rice, use aromatic herbs in the cooking pot. Try marjoram, mint, verbena, lime, rosemary, lemon or orange rind – or whatever you prefer.

steamed rice step-by-step

Serves **4**
180 g (6 oz) **rice**

Place the rice in a large bowl, cover with cold water and leave soaking for at least 1 hour, overnight if possible.

Drain the rice and place it in the upper compartment of a bamboo or stainless-steel steamer, wrapped in a clean cloth.

Bring the water in the lower compartment to boiling point, place the rice compartment on top, close the lid tightly and leave to cook for around 25 minutes.

pilaf rice

cooking by absorption

Heat a little butter or oil in a saucepan.
Add the rice and turn it in the fat until the
grains are well coated. Add the hot liquid
(water or stock) and cook, covered, for
about 12–15 minutes.

Allow on average 1 ½ times its volume of
water to 1 part of rice.

This method is suitable for nearly all kinds
of rice, especially long-grain.

butter or olive oil?

To coat the rice, you can use either a
knob of butter or olive oil, or even both.
The butter gives the rice a creamy texture
and the oil helps to cook it at higher
temperatures, so a blend is perfect if you
want rice that is both firm and creamy.

pilaf + spices

Flavour the cooking stock with 1 teaspoon
of ground turmeric and 1 teaspoon of
ground ginger; this gives the dish a
delicious aroma.

quick tip

Heat a lightly oiled saucepan then add
2 good pinches of curry powder and a
chopped onion. Blend well then add
300 g (10 oz) diced chicken fillets.
Cook, then serve with pilaf rice.

pilaf rice step-by-step

Serves **4**
1 tablespoon **olive oil**
180 g (6 oz) **rice**
300 ml (½ pint) **water** or **stock**
salt and **pepper**

Heat the oil in a saucepan. Add the rice and stir with a spatula until the grains are well coated in the oil.

Pour the water or stock over the rice, add seasoning and bring to simmering point, then cover and cook gently for 12–15 minutes.

Fluff up the grains of rice with a spatula.

risotto

This is a particularly delicious variant of pilaf cooking. However, it takes longer and the rice needs to be stirred constantly. Begin with the pilaf method: heat a little oil in a heavy-based saucepan, then add the rice and turn it, stirring until all the grains are well covered in oil. Next, add the hot stock, a ladleful at a time: first add a small quantity of stock and allow the grains to absorb the liquid.

Add another ladleful of stock and stir until absorbed before adding another one. Continue in this way until all the stock has been absorbed.

This cooking method requires some attention and patience.

take care!

A good risotto is cooked 'by ear'. You need to listen to the rice to judge the ideal time to add the stock. A risotto should simmer gently on the heat, never bubble. Parmesan cheese is added at the end of cooking, giving the rice its delicious creamy texture.

'mantecare!'

When the rice has finished cooking, add the butter and Parmesan and leave to rest for 1 or 2 minutes, then blend (mantecare) in rapidly with a wooden spoon. The whole art of a good risotto lies in this simple gesture.

arborio or carnaroli?

For preference, use 'superfino' arborio or carnaroli rice for risotto.

ideas for stock

Here there is plenty of choice. Depending on the recipe, you can use a vegetable or chicken stock or, for a more festive meal, a fish or game broth or maybe a veal stock.

risotto step-by-step

Serves **4**
2 tablespoons **olive oil**
200 g (7 oz) **short-grain rice**
1 litre (1¾ pints) **hot stock**
20 g (¾ oz) **butter**, diced
grated **Parmesan cheese**

Heat the oil in a heavy-based saucepan.
Sauté the rice for a few minutes then stir
it to ensure the grains are well coated
with the oil.

Add a ladleful of stock, allow the grains to absorb the liquid, then add another ladleful of stock. Continue in this way until all the stock has been absorbed.

Remove the pan of rice from the heat, add the butter and the grated Parmesan, then leave to rest for 1–2 minutes. Stir well.

sushi rice

Serves **4**
Preparation time **10 minutes**
  + 45 minutes resting time
Cooking time **12 minutes**

200 g (7 oz) **sushi rice**
250 ml (8 fl oz) **water**
80 ml (3 fl oz) **Japanese rice
  vinegar**
2 tablespoons **caster sugar**
½ teaspoon **salt**

Place the rice in a large bowl, cover it with cold water and stir it, using your fingers. Repeat this operation 2 or 3 times until all the water becomes clear.

Leave the rice to drain in a fine sieve for at least 30 minutes.

Place the rice and water in a small saucepan.

Bring to the boil, lower the heat, cover and cook for around 12 minutes. Take the pan off the heat and stand, covered, for 15 minutes.

Mix the rice vinegar, sugar and salt in a bowl.

Spread the rice over a large flat plate, sprinkle with the vinegar mixture and stir it in. If necessary, add more of the vinegar mixture. Cover with a damp cloth and leave to cool.

Now you can make one of the 4 recipes given on pages 104–111.

speedy gourmet rice

Here are some ways to enhance plain cooked rice or to flavour the water it's cooked in. They're simple and good!

rice with yogurt & mint

1 creamy **yogurt**
a few **mint leaves**, finely chopped
cooked rice
salt and **pepper**

Mix the yogurt and mint in a bowl.

Season lightly.

Place the warm rice in small bowls, cover with the mint-flavoured yogurt and serve immediately.

rice with roquefort sauce

100 g (3½ oz) **Roquefort cheese**, crumbled
100 ml (3½ fl oz) **crème fraîche**
2 tablespoons **white wine**
cooked rice
pepper

Melt the Roquefort with the crème fraîche and white wine for 5 minutes over a low heat.

Blend for 3 seconds in a food processor, add pepper and serve with steamed or boiled rice.

rice with parmesan flakes

shaved **Parmesan cheese**
cooked rice
pepper

Use a paring knife to shave flakes from a piece of Parmesan cheese.

Sprinkle the flakes over the rice, add plenty of pepper and serve immediately.

curried rice

1 teaspoon **mild curry**
  powder
rice
salt

Add the mild curry powder to salted cooking water, bring to simmering point, then pour in the rice.

Leave to cook gently, covered, for around 15 minutes.

rice with soy sauce

cooked rice
soy sauce

Place the warm rice in small bowls. Add a few drops of soy sauce to each bowl. Serve immediately.

rice with coconut milk

rice
coconut milk
grated rind of 1 **unwaxed lemon**
salt

Place the rice and the coconut milk, seasoned with salt and flavoured with the lemon rind, in a saucepan and cook, covered, for around 15 minutes.

Rest for 5 minutes before serving.

This rice goes very well with Indian dishes.

rice with chutney

cooked rice
1 teaspoon **chutney** of your choice

Place the warm rice in small bowls. Add 1 teaspoon of chutney and serve.

rice with orange rind

rice
orange juice
finely grated rind of 1 **orange**
pinch of **soft brown sugar**
salt

Cook the rice gently in a mixture of half salted water and half orange juice, for about 15 minutes, covered. Leave to rest for 15 minutes. Serve warm sprinkled with a little orange rind and brown sugar.

33

it's ready!

spiced spinach & mint pilaf

Serves **4**
Preparation time **10 minutes**
Cooking time **25 minutes**

3 tablespoons **vegetable oil**
180 g (6 oz) **basmati rice**
300 ml (½ pint) **vegetable** or
  chicken stock
1 teaspoon **cumin seeds**
200 g (7 oz) **spinach**, chopped
1 teaspoon grated **fresh root
  ginger**
1 **onion**, chopped
2 teaspoons **mint leaves**,
  chopped
salt and **pepper**

Heat 1 tablespoon of the oil in a heavy-based saucepan, then add the rice. Stir well to ensure the grains are well coated and translucent, then add the hot stock. Season, bring to simmering point, cover and cook over a low heat for 15 minutes.

Heat 1 tablespoon of the oil in a saucepan. Add the cumin seeds and let them brown, then add the spinach. Cook over a medium heat for 10 minutes, stirring regularly.

Meanwhile, heat the remaining oil in a saucepan, then add the ginger and onion. Cook until golden over a fairly high heat, stirring regularly to prevent them sticking to the pan.

Add the rice to the pan of spinach. Add the mint leaves, mix well and leave simmering for another few minutes. Season again, if necessary.

Serve hot, garnished with the fried onion and ginger.

For spiced spinach pilaf with preserved lemon, follow the recipe as above but omit the onion and ginger garnish. Instead, toast 50 g (2 oz) pine nuts in a small nonstick saucepan and fold them into the pilaf, with 1 tablespoon of diced preserved lemon, just before serving.

swordfish with star anise

Serves **4**
Preparation time **5 minutes**
  + 5 minutes resting time
Cooking time **15 minutes**

180 g (6 oz) **long-grain rice**
300 ml (½ pint) **hot water**
2 **star anise**
2 pinches of **chilli powder**
vegetable oil
4 **swordfish steaks**
salt and **pepper**

Rinse the rice in water and drain. Place in a heavy-based saucepan, cover with the hot water and add salt, the star anise and the chilli powder. Bring to a simmer, then cover and leave to cook over a gentle heat for around 15 minutes.

Remove the pan from the heat and leave to rest for 5 minutes without taking off the lid.

Meanwhile, oil the swordfish steaks lightly. Season them, then cook for 3–4 minutes on each side in a nonstick frying pan.

Remove the star anise from the dish of rice. Fluff up the grains with a fork. Serve immediately with the swordfish steaks.

For chicken with star anise, replace the swordfish with 4 chicken breast fillets. Heat 2 tablespoons of olive oil in a nonstick frying pan then cook the chicken breasts for around 6 minutes on each side. The chicken may be served diced, with a pinch of chopped fresh coriander.

sole minute with grapefruit

Serves **4**
Preparation time **5 minutes**
Cooking time **15 minutes**

½ **grapefruit**, juiced
1 teaspoon grated **fresh root ginger**
2 teaspoons **honey**
300 ml (½ pint) **water**
120 g (4 oz) **long-grain rice**
8 **fillets of sole**
salt and **pepper**

Place the grapefruit juice, grated ginger and honey in a small saucepan. Bring the mixture to boiling point, remove from the heat and leave, covered, to infuse.

Bring the water to the boil in a large saucepan. Add salt then the rice, stir, cover and lower the heat. Cook for around 12 minutes. The rice should be cooked but still retain some bite.

Heat some water in the lower pan of a steamer. Place the fillets of sole in the top compartment and cook for around 8 minutes.

Whisk the grapefruit, ginger and honey sauce then pour it lightly over the fillets of sole. Season then serve immediately with the rice. Ideally, serve the fish hot and the sauce cold.

For sole minute with warm mandarin sauce, replace the grapefruit juice with mandarin or orange juice. Follow the recipe as above but add a few mandarin segments to the infused sauce and warm it very gently just before serving with the fish.

spring vegetable & herb pilaf

Serves **4**

Preparation time **10 minutes**
 + 5 minutes resting time

Cooking time **20 minutes**

2 tablespoons **extra virgin
   olive oil**

1 **leek**, sliced

1 **courgette**, diced

grated rind and juice of
   1 **lemon**

2 **garlic cloves**, crushed

300 g (10 oz) **long-grain rice**

600 ml (1 pint) **hot
   vegetable stock**

150 g (5 oz) **green beans**,
   chopped

150 g (5 oz) fresh or frozen
   peas

4 tablespoons chopped **mixed
   herbs**, such as mint, parsley
   and chives

50 g (2 oz) **flaked almonds**,
   toasted

salt and **pepper**

Heat the oil in a large frying pan, add the leek, courgette, lemon rind, garlic and a little salt and pepper and cook gently over a medium-low heat for 5 minutes.

Add the rice, stir once and pour in the hot stock. Bring to the boil, then reduce the heat, cover and simmer gently for 10 minutes.

Stir in the beans and peas, cover and cook for a further 5 minutes.

Remove the pan from the heat and leave to rest for 5 minutes. Stir in the lemon juice and herbs and serve scattered with the flaked almonds.

For winter vegetable & fruit pilaf, heat 2 tablespoons of extra virgin olive oil in a large frying pan, add 1 sliced red onion, 1 teaspoon of ground coriander and 2 teaspoons of chopped thyme and cook gently over a medium-low heat for 5 minutes. Add 375 g (12 oz) diced pumpkin flesh with the rice as above, stir once and pour in the hot stock. Bring to the boil, then reduce the heat, cover and simmer gently for 10 minutes. Stir in 75 g (3 oz) raisins with the peas as above, cover and cook for 5 minutes. Remove the pan from the heat and leave to rest for 5 minutes. Stir in 2 tablespoons of chopped fresh coriander with the lemon juice and almonds.

pilaf rice with almonds & pine nuts

Serves **4**
Preparation time **5 minutes**
Cooking time **20 minutes**

1 tablespoon **vegetable oil**
180 g (6 oz) **long-grain rice**
300 ml (½ pint) **hot water**
100 g (3½ oz) **pine nuts**
100 g (3½ oz) **almonds**
salt and **pepper**

Heat the oil in a saucepan then add the rice. Coat the grains with oil, taking care to stir regularly with a spatula.

Pour the hot water over the rice, season, bring to a simmer, then cover and cook gently for around 15 minutes.

Meanwhile, toast the pine nuts lightly in a nonstick saucepan, followed by the almonds.

Serve the rice with the almonds and pine nuts.

For pilaf rice with sautéed beef & crunchy vegetables, cut 400 g (13 oz) beef in fine strips and stir-fry it in a saucepan or wok with 1 tablespoon of sesame oil. Then cook 400 g (13 oz) fresh vegetables (mangetout, fine beans, peas, baby carrots cut in strips diagonally). Add 2 teaspoons of sultanas. Serve hot with the almond and pine nut rice.

lemon-coconut rice

Serves **4**
Preparation time **5 minutes**
Cooking time **15 minutes**

180 g (6 oz) **basmati rice**
300 ml (½ pint) **hot water**
4 tablespoons **lemon juice**
1 **stick cinnamon**
pinch of **sugar**
vegetable oil, for oiling
40 g (1 ½ oz) grated
  coconut

Rinse the rice under running water several times. Place it in a saucepan, cover with the hot water and add the lemon juice, cinnamon stick and sugar. Bring to boiling point, cover and cook gently for around 15 minutes.

Heat a lightly oiled nonstick saucepan. Add the grated coconut and cook until golden, turning constantly with a wooden spatula.

Add the fried coconut to the rice just before serving.

For steamed cod balls to serve as an accompaniment, blend 200 g (7 oz) cod with a bunch of finely chopped coriander, 50 ml (2 fl oz) milk and 1 tablespoon of cornflour. Add 50 g (2 oz) spiced breadcrumbs. Shape the mixture into balls using your hands and steam for 8 minutes.

pilaf rice with chanterelle mushrooms

Serves **4**
Preparation time **15 minutes**
Cooking time **20 minutes**

250 g (8 oz) **chanterelles**
1 tablespoon **vegetable oil**
2 **shallots**, finely chopped
180 g (6 oz) **long-grain rice**
300 ml (½ pint) **chicken
  stock**
butter
2 tablespoons chopped
  parsley
salt and **pepper**

Clean the chanterelles carefully. Rinse them under a stream of cold water, drain quickly and dry well in a clean cloth.

Heat a tablespoon of oil in a saucepan and cook the shallots until golden.

Add the rice. Stir with a spatula until the grains are coated with the oil.

Pour the chicken stock over the rice, bring to a simmer, then cover and cook gently for around 15 minutes.

Melt a knob of butter in a nonstick saucepan and sauté the chanterelles in it for a few moments. Season and add the chopped parsley. Serve the rice with the sautéed mushrooms.

For pilaf rice with portobello mushrooms & tarragon, clean 250 g (8 oz) portobello mushrooms with a mushroom brush or dry kitchen paper and roughly chop or rip them into chunks. Sauté them in butter as above, then add 375 g (12 oz) shredded cooked chicken breast. Continue cooking for a few minutes to heat the chicken, then season and add 1 tablespoon of chopped tarragon.

crunchy rice persian-style

Serves **4–6**
Preparation time **15 minutes**
 + 3 hours soaking time
Cooking time **45 minutes**

500 g (1 lb) **basmati rice**
60 g (2½ oz) **butter**
pinch of **saffron threads**
salt

Wash the rice under running water several times then leave it to steep in a bowl of water for 3 hours.

Bring a large saucepan of salted water to the boil and add the drained rice in a stream. Cook for 5 minutes, or until tender on the outside and still firm inside; drain.

Melt the butter in a heavy-based saucepan and add the rice. Stir well then cover the pan tightly. Cook over a medium heat for 15 minutes. Lower the heat and continue cooking over a very, very low heat for a further 20 minutes.

Dissolve a pinch of saffron threads in 2 tablespoons of hot water. Take a bowlful of rice from the pan and sprinkle it with the saffron-flavoured water.

Place the remaining rice in a large serving dish and top it with a little dome of the saffron rice.

Scrape up the rice crusted around the bottom of the pan, and serve it separately on a small plate.

For fragrant crunchy rice, par-cook the rice as above. Sprinkle a small bowl of the rice with the saffron-flavoured water. Melt half the butter in a pan and stir in the saffron rice. Measure 2 teaspoons of advieh (Iranian spice mix). Layer the remaining rice in the pan, sprinkling each layer with a little advieh. Pour over 125 ml (4 fl oz) water and the remaining butter, melted. Cover pan tightly and cook as above. Serve garnished with 2 tablespoons each of dry-roasted pistachios and pomegranate seeds.

diced beef & rice with onions

Serves **4**
Preparation time **15 minutes**
Cooking time **10 minutes**

400 g (13 oz) **fillet** or **rump
beef steak**
2 tablespoons **soy sauce**
1 tablespoon **vegetable oil**
4 **onions**, chopped
400 g (13 oz) **cooked long-
grain rice**
pinch of **paprika powder**
salt and **pepper**

Chop the beef into small cubes. Sprinkle the soy sauce over the beef and mix in.

Heat the oil in a nonstick saucepan. Stir-fry the beef then season and set aside in a warm place.

Brown the chopped onions in the pan, add the cooked rice, sprinkle with the paprika and cook for a few minutes, stirring with a spatula.

Serve very hot with the cubed beef.

For diced turkey & rice with cashews, replace the beef with 400 g (13 oz) diced turkey breast. Follow the recipe as above, adding a few crushed cashew nuts when stir-frying the turkey.

sautéed chicken with sesame seeds

Serves **4**
Preparation time **5 minutes**
Cooking time **20 minutes**

2 tablespoons **vegetable oil**
180 g (6 oz) **long-grain rice**
300 ml (½ pint) **water**
500 g (1 lb) **chicken breast fillets**
4–5 tablespoons **sesame seeds**
handful of finely sliced **spring onions**
salt and **pepper**

Heat 1 tablespoon of the oil in a heavy-based saucepan then add the rice, stirring with a spatula to ensure that the grains are coated with oil. Add the water, season, bring to simmering point, then cover and cook gently for around 15 minutes.

Chop the chicken fillets into small, even-sized pieces and season to taste. Place the sesame seeds on a plate and toss the chicken in them.

Heat the remaining oil in a nonstick saucepan and cook the chicken for 4–5 minutes, stirring regularly so that it browns on all sides. Stir in the spring onions.

Serve the rice with the sesame diced chicken.

For prawn & cod dim sum, replace the chicken with 150 g (5 oz) raw peeled prawns and 350 g (11½ oz) cod. Stir-fry the prawns and the cod briefly in 1 tablespoon of oil, without cooking them fully. Process the mixture and shape into balls. Wrap the balls in spring roll wrappers that have been soaked in lukewarm water. Fry for 5–6 minutes then drain and serve hot with the rice.

rice with red wine & sautéed beef

Serves **4**
Preparation time **15 minutes**
Cooking time **20 minutes**

100 ml (3½ fl oz) **red wine**
200 ml (7 fl oz) **chicken stock**
1 tablespoon **vegetable oil**
2 **shallots**, chopped
180 g (6 oz) **long-grain rice**
2 **thyme sprigs**
600 g (1¼ lb) **beef fillet**, sliced
4 tablespoons finely chopped **flat-leaf parsley**
salt and **pepper**

Warm the wine and chicken stock in a saucepan.

Heat the oil in a flameproof dish and add the chopped shallots. Cook until they begin to change colour, stirring several times.

Add the rice and mix well so that the grains are well coated with the oil. Pour in the wine and stock. Season, add the thyme and bring to simmering point, then cover and cook in a preheated oven, 180°C (350°F), Gas Mark 4, for around 15 minutes.

Slice the beef fillet into 6 cm (2½ in) strips. Heat a nonstick saucepan and quickly sauté the strips of beef. Season, remove from the heat and sprinkle with the chopped parsley.

Serve the rice accompanied by the sautéed beef.

For orange & clove marinated beef, marinate the strips of beef for 3 hours in 500 ml (17 fl oz) red wine with the grated rind of 1 orange, 2 cloves and 5 black peppercorns. Drain the strips well before cooking. Sauté as above and serve with creole-style rice (see page 12). Garnish with 2 tablespoons of chopped thyme.

vegetable kebabs with pilaf

Serves **4**

Preparation time **20 minutes**
+ 20 minutes marinating and
10 minutes resting time

Cooking time **15 minutes**

1 tablespoon chopped
rosemary

5 tablespoons **extra virgin
olive oil**

2 **courgettes**

1 large **red pepper**, cored and
deseeded

16 **button mushrooms**,
trimmed

8 **cherry tomatoes**

Greek-style yogurt, to serve

Pilaf

250 g (8 oz) **basmati rice**

1 **onion**, finely chopped

2 **garlic cloves**, finely
chopped

6 **cardamom pods**, bruised

100 g (3½ oz) **dried
cranberries**

50 g (2 oz) **pistachios**,
toasted and chopped

2 tablespoons chopped **fresh
coriander**

salt and **pepper**

Soak 8 wooden skewers in cold water for 30 minutes.

Combine the rosemary with 2 tablespoons of the oil
and salt and pepper in a large bowl. Cut the courgettes
and red pepper into large pieces, add to the oil with the
mushrooms and tomatoes and toss well. Cover and leave
to marinate for 20 minutes.

Wash the rice under cold water, drain and put in a
saucepan. Add lightly salted water to cover the rice by
at least 5 cm (2 inches). Bring to the boil and boil for
10 minutes. Drain well.

Heat the remaining oil in a separate saucepan, add
the onion, garlic and cardamom pods and cook over
a medium heat, stirring frequently, for 5 minutes until
lightly golden. Add the rice, cranberries, pistachios,
coriander and salt and pepper. Stir well, then remove
from the heat, cover and leave to rest for 10 minutes.

Meanwhile, heat a ridged griddle pan until hot. Thread
the vegetables alternately on the skewers. Cook, turning
frequently, for 10 minutes until all the vegetables are
tender. Serve with the rice and Greek-style yogurt.

For mixed spice pilaf, cook the rice as above, adding
¼ teaspoon of saffron threads to the water. Cook
1 chopped onion and 2 crushed garlic cloves with
1 cinnamon stick and 6 cloves in 50 g (2 oz) butter for
5 minutes. Add the freshly cooked rice and stir lightly.
Remove from the heat, cover and stand for 10 minutes.
Remove the cinnamon stick and cloves before serving.

rice with leeks, ginger & cumin

Serves **4**
Preparation time **10 minutes**
Cooking time **10 minutes**

2 large **leeks**
1 tablespoon **olive oil**
1 teaspoon grated **fresh root ginger**
1 teaspoon **cumin powder**
400 g (13 oz) **cooked long-grain rice**
salt and **pepper**

Trim the leeks and wash carefully. Drain them and slice into thin rounds.

Heat the olive oil in a large nonstick saucepan. Add the grated ginger, turn with a spoon, then add the cumin powder. Add the sliced leeks, season and cook for around 10 minutes, stirring regularly. If necessary, add 1 or 2 tablespoons of water to keep the mixture from sticking. Season to taste.

Add the cooked rice to the pan and fluff up the grains with a fork. Serve hot.

For rice with leeks, fennel & lemon, omit the cumin powder. Cook 1 bulb of fennel, cut into quarters and sliced, with the ginger and leeks. Stir in the grated rind of 1 lemon with the seasoning just before adding the rice.

steamed rice with sage

Serves **4–6**

Preparation time **5 minutes** +
  1 hour steeping time

Cooking time **20 minutes**

200 g (7 oz) **long-grain rice**
4 **sage leaves**
salt and **pepper**

Place the rice in a large bowl and cover with cold water. Leave to steep for at least 1 hour, then drain.

Place water in the lower compartment of a steamer, add the sage leaves and bring to simmering point. Place the rice in the top compartment. Cover and cook for around 20 minutes. Season and serve hot.

For lamb gratin with sage, sauté around 10 pieces of neck of lamb in a saucepan until they begin to colour. Set aside in an ovenproof dish. Sauté a sliced onion and 6 small carrots, cut into batons, in the pan for 3 minutes. Add them to the ovenproof dish along with 3 small white turnips, cubed, 3 diced tomatoes, 4 sage leaves and 2 garlic cloves. Cover with a good vegetable stock, then season and place in a preheated oven, 180°C (350°F), Gas Mark 4, for around 45 minutes. Serve with rice steamed with sage.

lemon & basil rice

Serves **4–6**
Preparation time **10 minutes**
Cooking time **20 minutes**

1 tablespoon **vegetable oil**
180 g (6 oz) **long-grain rice**
300 ml (½ pint) **chicken stock**
4 tablespoons chopped **parsley**
4 tablespoons chopped **basil**
grated rind of 2 **unwaxed lemons**
50 g (2 oz) **Parmesan cheese**, freshly grated
salt and **pepper**

Heat the oil in a saucepan, add the rice and turn it, stirring regularly until the grains are fully coated in the oil and become transparent.

Warm the chicken stock and pour it over the rice. Add the parsley, basil and grated lemon rind. Season and cook, covered, for around 15 minutes over a gentle heat.

Serve hot, with the grated Parmesan cheese.

For lemon & basil monkfish, slice 2 courgettes lengthwise into very thin strips. Sprinkle some torn basil leaves and grated lemon rind over 4–6 monkfish fillets and season to taste. Wrap the courgette strips around the fish. Sprinkle lightly with salt and pepper, then heat some olive oil in a saucepan and cook the fish gently for around 7–8 minutes, turning once. Serve with the lemon and basil rice.

salads

goats' cheese salad with walnuts

Serves **4**
Preparation time **10 minutes**
Cooking time **15 minutes**

120 g (4 oz) **long-grain rice**
1 **goats' cheese**, slightly dry
1 **lettuce heart**
large handful of shelled
  walnuts
1 tablespoon chopped **chives**

Vinaigrette
1 tablespoon **wine vinegar**
1 tablespoon **tapenade**
3 tablespoons **olive oil**
grated rind of 1 **unwaxed**
  lemon
salt and **pepper**

Cook the rice creole-style (see page 12) for 15 minutes in plenty of water; it should be cooked but still retain some bite. Pour it into a sieve and stop the cooking by rinsing under cold running water, drain thoroughly and leave to cool.

Remove the skin from the goats' cheese and slice it.

Make the vinaigrette: blend the vinegar into the tapenade, salt it lightly then whisk. Add the olive oil little by little then incorporate the grated lemon rind and a little pepper.

Arrange the rice in a large bowl then add the sliced goats' cheese, lettuce leaves, shelled walnuts, chopped chives and vinaigrette. Season with salt and pepper.

For feta & kalamata salad with oregano, replace the goats' cheese with 125 g (4 oz) crumbled feta. Add a few finely chopped black olives, such as kalamatas, and replace the chives with chopped fresh oregano.

mixed-leaf salad with pine nuts

Serves **4**
Preparation time **10 minutes**
Cooking time **15 minutes**

120 g (4 oz) **long-grain rice**
50 g (2 oz) **mixed salad
  leaves**
12 small **cherry tomatoes**
1 small **celery stick**, diced
a little grated **Parmesan
  cheese**
30 g (1¼ oz) **pine nuts**
5 **basil leaves**, chopped

Vinaigrette
1 tablespoon **wine vinegar**
3 tablespoons **olive oil**
salt and **pepper**

Cook the rice creole-style (see page 12). It should retain a slightly firm texture. Pour it into a sieve and stop the cooking by rinsing under cold running water, drain thoroughly and leave to cool.

Arrange the rice and salad leaves in a large bowl. Add the cherry tomatoes, diced celery, grated Parmesan and pine nuts.

Make the vinaigrette: mix the vinegar and a pinch of salt in a bowl. Add the olive oil drop by drop, whisking all the time, then drizzle over the salad. Just before serving, sprinkle with the chopped basil leaves.

For chicken & Gruyère wraps to accompany the salad, pan-fry 2 chicken breast fillets, then cut into small dice. Spread tapenade over 4 wraps, add the diced chicken and roll up the wraps, folding over the ends to seal tightly. Arrange in a lightly greased ovenproof dish, sprinkle with grated Gruyère cheese and flash under the grill for 5 minutes.

sushi rice salad

Serves **2–3**
Preparation time **10 minutes**
 + 45 minutes resting time
Cooking time **12 minutes**

250 g (8 oz) **sushi rice**
6 tablespoons **rice wine
 vinegar**
2½ tablespoons **caster sugar**
5 g (¼ oz) **pickled ginger**,
 chopped
½ teaspoon **wasabi**
½ **cucumber**
1 **avocado**, about 175 g
 (6 oz), peeled and cut into
 small cubes
250 g (8 oz) **skinless
 salmon**, cut into bite-sized
 pieces
8 **spring onions**, finely sliced
3 tablespoons toasted
 sesame seeds, to garnish

Cook the sushi rice according to the instructions on page 26, and leave to stand.

Meanwhile, put the vinegar and sugar in a small saucepan and heat gently, stirring, until the sugar has dissolved. Turn off the heat and add the chopped pickled ginger and wasabi. Leave to cool. Cut the cucumber in half lengthways and scoop out the seeds with a teaspoon. Slice the flesh finely and add to the cooled vinegar mix.

Transfer the cooked rice to a dish, strain the vinegar mixture over it, reserving the cucumber, stir and leave to cool.

Place the cooled rice in a large salad bowl and combine gently with the cucumber, avocado, salmon and spring onions. Top with toasted sesame seeds and serve.

For seared tuna & sushi rice salad, mix 2 tablespoons of soy sauce with ¼ teaspoon of wasabi and brush 300 g (10 oz) tuna loin with the mixture. Roll the tuna in sesame seeds until coated all over. Heat 1 tablespoon of vegetable oil in a large frying pan over a high heat and fry the tuna for 1–2 minutes on each side. Remove the tuna from the heat and allow to rest. Prepare the salad as above but omit the salmon. Thinly slice the tuna and serve with the sushi rice salad.

creamy chicory & olive salad

Serves **4**
Preparation time **10 minutes**
Cooking time **15 minutes**

120 g (4 oz) **long-grain rice**
3 large **chicory heads**
12 **black olives**
grated rind of 1 **unwaxed orange**
2 teaspoons **lemon juice**
3 tablespoons **crème fraîche**
salt and **pepper**

Cook the rice creole-style for 15 minutes in plenty of boiling water (see page 12). The rice should be cooked but still retain some bite. Drain it into a sieve and stop the cooking by rinsing under cold running water. Drain well and leave to cool.

Wash the chicory heads and dry them in a clean cloth, then chop finely.

Arrange the rice and chicory in a large salad dish. Add the olives and grated orange rind.

Place the lemon juice and crème fraîche in a bowl. Sprinkle with salt and pepper to taste, then whisk rapidly. Drizzle the creamy sauce over the salad just before serving.

For artichoke & olive salad, replace the chicory with 4 artichoke hearts bottled in oil, well drained and finely chopped. Use green olives instead of black and replace the grated orange rind with 1 teaspoon of rinsed, dried and finely chopped preserved lemon.

wild rice salad with smoked salmon

Serves **4**
Preparation time **10 minutes**
Cooking time **45 minutes**

300 ml (½ pint) **water**
125 g (4 oz) **wild rice**
200 g (7 oz) **smoked
    salmon**, sliced into ribbons
1 tablespoon toasted
    sesame seeds
salt and **pepper**

Vinaigrette
½ teaspoon **fine Dijon
    mustard**
1 tablespoon **cider vinegar**
3 tablespoons **sunflower oil**
1 tablespoon **maple syrup**
1 tablespoon **soy sauce**
salt and **pepper**

Bring the water to the boil. Add salt, pour in the rice and stir well. Cover and cook gently for 45 minutes. The rice should be cooked but still retain some bite. Pour it into a sieve and stop the cooking by rinsing under cold running water, drain thoroughly and leave to cool.

Make the vinaigrette: place the mustard in a bowl, then add the cider vinegar, sunflower oil, maple syrup and soy sauce. Blend well and season with salt and pepper.

Arrange the cold wild rice in a salad dish and spread the sliced smoked salmon over it. Drizzle over the sauce and sprinkle with sesame seeds and some ground pepper.

For wild rice salad with smoked chicken, replace the smoked salmon with 200 g (7 oz) shredded smoked chicken breast. Replace the soy sauce in the vinaigrette with the grated rind and juice of 1 lime and add 2 tablespoons of chopped coriander.

citrussy rice salad

Serves **4**
Preparation time **15 minutes**
Cooking time **15 minutes**

120 g (4 oz) **long-grain rice**
1 **orange**
1 **grapefruit**
1 tablespoon chopped **fresh
   herbs** (parsley, chives,
   tarragon, chervil)
12 dry-roasted **pistachios**

Sauce
6 tablespoons **orange juice**
5 tablespoons **grapefruit
   juice**
1 tablespoon **honey**
2 tablespoons **sunflower oil**
1 teaspoon grated fresh
   root ginger
salt and **pepper**

Cook the rice creole-style for 15 minutes in plenty of boiling water (see page 12). It should be cooked but still retain some bite. Pour it into a sieve and stop the cooking by rinsing under cold running water, drain thoroughly and leave to cool.

Peel the orange and grapefruit. Remove the pith and cut the flesh into large dice.

Place the rice in a large salad bowl then add the diced orange and grapefruit.

Make the sauce: whisk together the orange juice, grapefruit juice, honey and sunflower oil. Season with salt and pepper. Add the grated ginger and stir well.

Drizzle the sauce over the rice salad. Sprinkle with the chopped herbs and decorate with the pistachios.

For citrus & prawn salad, cook 6 peeled, sliced king prawns in a little fish or vegetable stock, lightly seasoned with paprika and salt, and fold them into the rice with the citrus fruits.

cherry & sun-dried tomatoes

Serves **4**
Preparation time **10 minutes**
Cooking time **15 minutes**

300 ml (½ pint) **water**
120 g (4 oz) **long-grain rice**
12 **cherry tomatoes**
100 g (3½ oz) **sun-dried tomatoes in oil**
1 small **red onion**
10 small **black olives**
5 **basil leaves**
100 g (3½ oz) **cooked mangetout**
salt and pepper

Vinaigrette
1 tablespoon **balsamic vinegar**
1 teaspoon **mustard**
3 tablespoons **basil-flavoured olive oil**
salt

Bring the water to the boil. Add salt, pour in the rice and stir. Cover and lower the heat. Cook gently for around 15 minutes. The rice should be cooked but still retain some bite. Pour it into a sieve and stop the cooking by rinsing under cold running water, drain thoroughly and leave to cool.

Rinse the cherry tomatoes and carefully wipe them dry. Drain the sun-dried tomatoes and cut them into fine strips. Thinly slice the red onion. Rinse and pit the olives. Wash the basil leaves and shred finely.

Make the vinaigrette: place the vinegar in a bowl and add the mustard, olive oil and salt. Whisk rapidly.

Arrange the rice, mangetout, cherry tomatoes and sun-dried tomato strips in a salad bowl. Add the onion, olives and basil; drizzle with the vinaigrette and garnish with a good grinding of pepper. Serve well chilled.

For Niçoise-style salad, scatter some chunks of canned tuna and 2 hard-boiled eggs cut into wedges over the rice. Add a few salted anchovies, rinsed thoroughly under cold running water and patted dry with kitchen paper. Replace the basil leaves with 1 tablespoon of chopped parsley and the mangetout with French beans. For the vinaigrette, use red wine vinegar instead of balsamic and garlic-flavoured olive oil instead of basil-flavoured.

fennel & apple salad

Serves **4**
Preparation time **15 minutes**
Cooking time **15 minutes**

300 ml (½ pint) **water**
120 g (4 oz) **long-grain rice**
2 small **fennel bulbs**
3 **sharp apples,** such as
  Granny Smith
juice of 1 **lime**
salt

Bring the water to the boil in a large saucepan. Add salt, pour in the rice and stir. Cover and lower the heat. Cook gently for around 15 minutes. The rice should be cooked but still retain some bite. Pour it into a sieve and stop the cooking by rinsing under cold running water, drain thoroughly and leave to cool.

Wash the fennel. Quarter the bulbs then dice finely. Peel and quarter the apples, remove the pips and chop into very small dice. Sprinkle the fennel and apples with the lime juice.

Arrange the diced fennel and apple in a salad bowl, along with the rice.

For fennel & goats' cheese cocktail, place some rice in 4 small glass dishes and top with fennel-apple salad. Scatter over 2 teaspoons of soft goats' cheese. Garnish with crushed walnuts or a few thin slices of closed-cup baby mushrooms lightly seasoned with lemon juice.

apple, pear & walnut salad

Serves **4**
Preparation time **10 minutes**
Cooking time **15 minutes**

300 ml (½ pint) **water**
120 g (4 oz) **long-grain rice**
2 **sharp apples**
2 **pears**
grated rind and juice of
  1 **unwaxed lemon**
handful of shelled **walnuts**
salt

Vinaigrette
1 teaspoon **wholegrain
  mustard**
1 tablespoon **cider vinegar**
1 tablespoon **walnut oil**
2 tablespoons **sunflower oil**
salt and **pepper**

Bring the water to the boil in a large saucepan. Add salt and pour in the rice. Stir, then cover and lower the heat. Cook gently for around 15 minutes. The rice should be cooked but still retain some bite. Pour it into a sieve and stop the cooking by rinsing under cold running water, drain thoroughly and leave to cool.

Peel the apples and pears, remove the pips and dice the fruit finely. Sprinkle with lemon juice.

Make the vinaigrette: place the wholegrain mustard in a bowl, incorporate the vinegar and a little salt, whisk and add the 2 oils drop by drop, stirring all the time. Add pepper.

Arrange the rice, diced apples and pears and finally the shelled walnuts in a large bowl. Top with the grated lemon rind and the vinaigrette.

For peach salad with Parma ham, use wild rice, cooked as above but for 45 minutes. Substitute the apples and pears with 2 chopped ripe peaches, sprinkled with lemon juice (remove the skins by blanching the peaches in boiling water for 30 seconds, then plunging them immediately into iced water – the skins should slip off easily). Arrange the rice, peaches, Parma ham and shelled walnuts in a large bowl and top with the grated lemon rind and the vinaigrette.

feta & kalamata olives in vinaigrette

Serves **4**
Preparation time **10 minutes**
Cooking time **15 minutes**

300 ml (½ pint) **water**
120 g (4 oz) **long-grain rice**
4 **tomatoes**
1 **white onion**
1 **garlic clove**
200 g (7 oz) **feta cheese**
20 **kalamata olives**
1 tablespoon **capers in
    vinegar**
4 tablespoons finely
    chopped **parsley**
a few **basil leaves**
salt

Vinaigrette
1 tablespoon **white wine
    vinegar**
3 tablespoons **olive oil**
pinch of fresh **thyme**
salt and **pepper**

Bring the water to boiling point in a large saucepan.
Add salt then pour in the rice and stir. Cover and lower
the heat. Cook gently for around 15 minutes. The rice
should be cooked but still retain some bite. Pour it into a
sieve and stop the cooking by rinsing under cold running
water, drain thoroughly and leave to cool.

Wash and dry the tomatoes. Chop into large dice. Peel
and chop the onion and garlic. Cut the feta into small
cubes. Slice the olives into small strips. Drain the capers.

Place the rice in a salad bowl. Top with the tomato,
onion, garlic, diced feta, olives, capers and chopped
parsley.

Make the vinaigrette: mix the vinegar with a pinch of
salt then add the olive oil drop by drop, whisking all the
time. Add a pinch of thyme and drizzle over the salad.
Grind a little pepper over it.

Rinse and dry the basil leaves, then shred finely. Arrange
over the salad just before serving.

**For feta & kalamata olives in honey & mustard
dressing**, whisk together 2 teaspoons of wholegrain
mustard, 2 teaspoons of clear honey and 2 tablespoons
of white wine vinegar. Add 3 tablespoons of olive oil drop
by drop, whisking all the time as if for a mayonnaise.
Drizzle over the salad as above, omitting the thyme.

spicy fried rice with spinach salad

Serves **3–4**
Preparation time **10 minutes**
Cooking time **10 minutes**

4 **eggs**
2 tablespoons **sherry**
2 tablespoons **light soy sauce**
1 bunch of **spring onions**
4 tablespoons **groundnut oil**
75 g (3 oz) **unsalted cashew nuts**
1 **green pepper**, deseeded and finely chopped
½ teaspoon **Chinese five-spice powder**
250 g (8 oz) **cooked long-grain rice**
150 g (5 oz) **baby spinach**
100 g (3½ oz) **bean sprouts** or 50 g (2 oz) **pea shoots**
salt and **pepper**
sweet chilli sauce, to serve

Beat the eggs with the sherry and 1 tablespoon of the soy sauce in a small bowl. Cut 2 of the spring onions into 7 cm (3 inch) lengths, then cut lengthways into fine shreds. Leave in a bowl of very cold water to curl up slightly. Finely chop the remaining spring onions, keeping the white and green parts separate.

Heat half the oil in a large frying pan or wok and fry the cashew nuts and green parts of the spring onions, turning in the oil, until the cashew nuts are lightly browned. Drain with a slotted spoon.

Add the white parts of the spring onions to the pan and stir-fry for 1 minute. Add the beaten eggs and cook, stirring constantly, until the egg starts to scramble into small pieces, rather than 1 omelette.

Stir in the green pepper and five-spice powder with the remaining oil and cook for 1 minute, then tip in the cooked rice and spinach with the remaining soy sauce, mixing the ingredients together well until thoroughly combined and the spinach has wilted.

Return the cashew nuts and spring onions to the pan with the bean sprouts or pea shoots and season to taste. Pile on to serving plates, scatter with the drained spring onion curls and serve with sweet chilli sauce.

For spicy fried rice with baby corn, replace the spinach with ½ small Chinese cabbage, shredded, and 200 g (7 oz) baby corn, sliced, and add to the pan with the green pepper.

wild rice & turkey salad

Serves **4**
Preparation time **10 minutes**
 + cooling time
Cooking time **50 minutes**

300 g (10 oz) **wild rice**
2 **green apples**, finely sliced
75 g (3 oz) **pecan nuts**
rind and juice of 2 **oranges**
60 g (2¼ oz) **cranberries**
3 tablespoons **olive oil**
2 tablespoons chopped
 parsley
4 **turkey fillets**, each about
 125 g (4 oz)
salt and **pepper**

Bring the water to the boil. Add salt, pour in the rice and stir well. Cover and cook gently for 45 minutes. The rice should be cooked but still retain some bite. Pour it into a sieve and stop the cooking by rinsing under cold running water, drain thoroughly and leave to cool.

Mix the apples into the rice with the pecans, the orange rind and juice and the cranberries. Season to taste with salt and pepper.

Mix together the oil and parsley. Cut the turkey fillets into halves or thirds lengthways and cover with this mixture. Heat a frying pan until it is hot but not smoking and cook the turkey for 2 minutes on each side. Slice the turkey, arrange the pieces next to the rice salad and serve immediately.

For sticky citrus pork chops with wild rice salad, whisk the rind and juice of 1 orange, 2 tablespoons of orange marmalade, 1 tablespoon of soy sauce and 1 tablespoon of sweet chilli sauce. Heat a large frying pan over a high heat and seal 4 pork chops, each about 175 g (6 oz), for 2 minutes on each side. Put the chops on a foil-lined baking sheet and cover with the marinade. Cook in a preheated oven, 180°C (350°F), Gas Mark 4, for 10–15 minutes until cooked through. Prepare the salad as above and serve topped with the pork chops.

chicken rice salad

Serves **4**

Preparation time **10 minutes**
  + cooling time

Cooking time **12 minutes**

4 **chicken thighs**, skinned
  and boned
175 g (6 oz) **long-grain rice**
2 teaspoons **lemon juice**
2 tablespoons **peanut
  butter** (optional)
2 tablespoons **olive oil**
2 **pineapple rings**, chopped
1 **red pepper**, cored,
  deseeded and chopped
75 g (3 oz) **sugar snap peas**,
  sliced
4 tablespoons **peanuts**
  (optional)

Place the chicken thighs in a steamer set over boiling water for 10–12 minutes until cooked through. Alternatively, simmer them in shallow water in a frying pan for 10 minutes. Remove from the steamer or pan and set aside to cool.

Meanwhile, cook the rice in a large saucepan of boiling water for 12 minutes. Drain and rinse under cold water to cool the rice completely, then tip it into a large bowl.

Make the dressing: mix together the lemon juice and peanut butter, if using, until well combined, then whisk in the oil.

Dice the chicken thighs into bite-sized pieces and stir into the rice. Add the pineapple, red pepper, sugar snap peas and peanuts, if using. Pour the dressing over the chicken rice salad and serve.

For prawn rice salad, make up the peanut dressing as above. Replace the chicken with 150 g (5 oz) peeled cooked prawns tossed with 2 tablespoons of toasted sesame seeds. Cut ¼ cucumber into thin sticks and toss with the rice, peanut sauce, prawns and seeds.

finger food

rice balls with coconut milk

Serves **4–6**
Preparation time **5 minutes**
 + 1 hour steeping time
Cooking time **10 minutes**

200 g (7 oz) **sticky rice**
120 ml (4 fl oz) **coconut milk**
pinch of **salt**

Place the rice in a large bowl and add water to cover. Leave to steep for at least 1 hour, then drain and turn it out on a clean cloth.

Heat the water in the bottom compartment of a rice-cooker or steamer. Place the cloth containing the rice in the upper compartment. Cover and steam for 10 minutes.

Open the cloth, let the rice cool for 1 minute then turn it into a deep dish.

Pour over the coconut milk, sprinkle with salt and serve warm.

Use small coffee cups as moulds for the rice then turn out the little domes of rice onto small plates.

Eat with your fingers or a small spoon.

For rice balls with coconut & mango, chop the flesh of a quarter of a mango into fine dice and stir into the cooked rice before adding the coconut milk and salt. Pack the rice into small moulds and place in the refrigerator until well chilled. To serve, turn out onto small plates and garnish with a sliver of mango.

prawn spring rolls

Serves **4**
Preparation time **25 minutes**
  + 15 minutes soaking time
Cooking time **5 minutes**

30 g (1¼ oz) **rice thread noodles**
200 g (7 oz) **raw peeled prawns**
200 g (7 oz) **chicken breast**
1 **carrot**, grated
1 **garlic clove**, chopped
1 tablespoon grated **coconut**
12 **spring roll wrappers**
vegetable oil
salt and **pepper**
fresh mint sprigs and **spicy sauce**, to serve

Place the rice noodles in a bowl, cover with warm water and leave to soak for 15 minutes. Cook for 3 minutes in a saucepan of boiling salted water, then drain.

Chop the prawns and chicken breast finely and turn them into a large bowl. Add the noodles, grated carrot, chopped garlic and coconut and mix in well. Season and stir again.

Soften the spring roll wrappers by dipping them briefly in a plate of lightly sugared water, then wipe off the moisture and lay them flat on the work-surface. Place some stuffing on each wrapper, fold the edges in towards the filling and roll up tightly.

Deep-fry the rolls in very hot vegetable oil and drain on kitchen paper.

Serve warm with some fresh mint and a spicy sauce.

For langoustine spring rolls, replace the prawns with 200 g (7 oz) langoustine (Dublin Bay prawns) and the chicken breast with 200 g (7 oz) turkey breast. Add ½ teaspoon of crushed dried red chilli to the filling mixture.

chicken spring rolls

Serves **4**

Preparation time **35 minutes**
 + 30 minutes soaking time

Cooking time **5 minutes**

4 **fragrant black
  mushrooms**
40 g (1 ½ oz) **rice thread
  noodles**
200 g (7 oz) **pork fillet,** diced
200 g (7 oz) **chicken breast,**
  diced
1 **carrot**, grated
1 **garlic clove**, chopped
1 teaspoon grated **fresh root
  ginger**
1 tablespoon **nuoc-mâm**
  (Vietnamese fish sauce)
12 **spring roll wrappers**
vegetable oil
salt and **pepper**
lettuce leaves and **spicy
  sauce**, to serve

Soak the black mushrooms in a bowl of warm water for around 30 minutes. Drain and dry them, then chop finely.

Place the rice noodles in a large bowl, cover with warm water and leave to steep for 15 minutes. Cook for 3 minutes in a saucepan of boiling salted water. Drain.

Place the pork, chicken, rice noodles, mushrooms, carrot, garlic, ginger and nuoc-mâm in a large bowl. Season and mix well.

Soften the spring roll wrappers by dipping them briefly in a plate of lightly sugared water, then wipe off the moisture and lay them flat on the work-surface. Place some stuffing on each wrapper, fold the edges in towards the filling and roll up tightly.

Fry the spring rolls in very hot vegetable oil and drain on kitchen paper.

Serve the warm spring rolls with a few salad leaves and a spicy sauce.

For pork & prawn spring rolls, replace the chicken with 200 g (7 oz) raw peeled prawns, chopped. Replace the black mushrooms with 4 fresh chanterelle mushrooms. Rinse them under a stream of cold water, drain quickly and dry well in a clean cloth, then chop finely.

shrimp spring rolls with mint

Serves **4**
Preparation time **25 minutes**
  + 15 minutes soaking time
Cooking time **3 minutes**

40 g (1 ½ oz) **rice thread noodles**
a few **green salad leaves**
50 g (2 oz) **bean sprouts**
12 **spring roll wrappers**
150 g (5 oz) grated **carrot**
200 g (7 oz) **peeled cooked shrimps**
2 tablespoons finely chopped **mint**
1 tablespoon finely chopped **coriander leaves**
a few sliced **spring onions**
chilli sauce, sweet or strong, according to taste, to serve

Place the rice noodles in a large bowl, cover with warm water and leave to steep for 15 minutes. Cook for 3 minutes in a saucepan of boiling salted water. Drain.

Wash and dry the salad leaves and bean sprouts.

Soften the spring roll wrappers by dipping them briefly in a plate of lightly sugared water, then wipe off the moisture and lay them flat on the work-surface.

Place a little grated carrot, some shrimps, noodles, a few bean sprouts and a sprinkling of mint and coriander on each wrapper. Fold the sides towards the middle and roll the spring rolls up tightly.

Tuck a sliver of spring onion into the top of each spring roll and serve with chilli sauce.

For smoked duck spring rolls, replace the shrimps with 200 g (7 oz) finely shredded smoked duck breast. Replace the mint with 1 tablespoon of finely chopped Thai basil and 1 tablespoon of finely chopped sage leaves.

salmon & dill cornets

Serves **4**
Preparation time **10 minutes**
  + 45 minutes resting time
Cooking time **12 minutes**

Rice
200 g (7 oz) **sushi rice**
250 ml (8 fl oz) **water**
80 ml (3 fl oz) **Japanese rice vinegar**
2 tablespoons **caster sugar**
½ teaspoon **salt**

Garnish
6 sheets of **nori**
250 g (8 oz) **smoked salmon**
Japanese soy sauce (shoyu)
wasabi paste
Japanese pickled ginger (gari)
a few **dill sprigs**

Make the sushi rice (see page 26).

Cut the sheets of nori into 4 pieces.

Slice the smoked salmon into strips.

Place the soy sauce, wasabi paste, pickled ginger and dill sprigs in separate serving bowls.

Arrange the nori strips and the sliced salmon on a plate.

Let everyone make their own cornets by spreading rice on the nori sheets, then adding a touch of wasabi and a little ginger and dill before rolling them into cornets and dipping briefly in the soy sauce.

For smoked salmon & avocado cornets, peel an avocado and slice it into strips. Sprinkle with the juice of 1 lemon and arrange on the plate with the nori and salmon. Replace the dill with baby watercress leaves.

cornets with fish roe

Serves **4**
Preparation time **45 minutes**
   + 10 minutes resting time
Cooking time **12 minutes**

Rice
200 g (7 oz) **sushi rice**
250 ml (8 fl oz) **water**
80 ml (3 fl oz) **Japanese rice
   vinegar**
2 tablespoons **caster sugar**
½ teaspoon **salt**

Garnish
6 sheets of **nori**
Japanese soy sauce (shoyu)
wasabi paste
Japanese pickled ginger
   (gari)
a few **basil leaves**
200 g (7 oz) **salmon roe** or
   cod roe

Make the sushi rice (see page 26).

Cut the sheets of nori into 4 pieces.

Place the soy sauce, wasabi paste, pickled ginger and basil leaves in separate serving bowls.

Arrange the nori leaves and fish roe on a plate.

Let everyone make their own cornets by spreading rice on the nori sheets, then adding a touch of wasabi and a little garnish before rolling them into cornets and dipping briefly in the soy sauce.

For raw fish cornets, replace the fish roe with 200 g (7 oz) very thinly sliced sashimi-grade yellowfin tuna, seasoned with a little Sichuan pepper. Replace the basil with coriander microgreens.

avocado & crab cornets

Serves **4**
Preparation time **10 minutes**
   + 45 minutes resting time
Cooking time **12 minutes**

Rice
200 g (7 oz) **sushi rice**
250 ml (8 fl oz) **water**
80 ml (3 fl oz) **Japanese rice vinegar**
2 tablespoons **caster sugar**
½ teaspoon **salt**

Garnish
6 sheets of **nori**
1 **avocado**
juice of 1 **lemon**
Japanese soy sauce (shoyu)
wasabi paste
Japanese pickled ginger (gari)
100 g (4 oz) **crabmeat**, cooked and shelled

Prepare the sushi rice (see page 26).

Cut the sheets of nori into 4 pieces.

Peel the avocado and slice it into strips. Sprinkle with the lemon juice.

Place the soy sauce, wasabi paste and pickled ginger into small separate bowls.

Arrange the nori sheets, avocado strips and crabmeat on a plate.

Let everyone make their own cornets by spreading rice on the nori sheets and adding a touch of wasabi and a little garnish before rolling them into cornets and dipping in the soy sauce.

For avocado & smoked chicken cornets, replace the crabmeat with 100 g (3½ oz) finely shredded smoked chicken breast. Replace the lemon juice with the juice of 2 limes.

vegetarian cornets

Serves **4**
Preparation time **10 minutes**
  + 45 minutes resting time
Cooking time **12 minutes**

Rice
200 g (7 oz) **sushi rice**
250 ml (8 fl oz) **water**
80 ml (3 fl oz) **Japanese rice vinegar**
2 tablespoons **caster sugar**
½ teaspoon **salt**

Garnish
6 sheets of **nori**
1 **cucumber**
Japanese soy sauce (shoyu)
wasabi paste
Japanese pickled ginger (gari)
12 **basil leaves**
2 tablespoons toasted **sesame seeds**

Prepare the sushi rice (see page 26).

Cut the sheets of nori into 4 pieces.

Wash the cucumber and cut it in half lengthways then slice into 4 cm (1½ inch) strips.

Place a little soy sauce in serving bowls then divide the wasabi paste, the pickled ginger, the basil leaves and the sesame seeds among them.

Arrange the nori sheets and strips of cucumber on a plate.

Let everyone make their own cornets by spreading rice on the nori sheets, then adding cucumber before rolling the cornets and dipping them in the soy sauce.

For tofu & aubergine cornets, cut 100 g (3½ oz) smoked tofu into thin slivers and arrange them on the plate with the nori. Cut a small aubergine into thin slices lengthways then brush each slice lightly with oil on both sides and griddle or pan-fry until golden. Cut into thin slivers and serve in place of the strips of cucumber.

lemon vine leaves

Serves **4–6**
Preparation time **35 minutes**
Cooking time **1 hour**

200 g (7 oz) **short-grain rice**
300 g (10 oz) **minced lamb**
3 **mint leaves**, finely chopped
1 bunch of **flat leaf parsley**,
    finely chopped
finely grated rind of 1 **lemon**
1 **onion**
1 tablespoon **olive oil**
3 **garlic cloves**, peeled
250 g (8 oz) **vine leaves**
1 litre (1¾ pints) **hot**
    vegetable stock
juice of 2 **lemons**
pinch of **ground cinnamon**
salt and **pepper**

Rinse the rice well under cold running water.

Mix together the lamb, mint, parsley and grated lemon rind. Season generously then blend again.

Peel and finely chop the onion.

Heat the olive oil in a nonstick saucepan, add the onion and let it colour. Add the rice and turn in the oil until it becomes transparent. Add the lamb stuffing ingredients. Stir, then cook for around 5 minutes.

Rinse and drain the vine leaves then spread them out flat on a work-surface. Spoon a dollop of stuffing in the middle of each vine leaf, then fold in the edges and roll the leaf up tightly. Prepare the other leaves in the same way.

Arrange the stuffed vine leaves in a saucepan. Add the garlic cloves and the hot stock, with water to cover if necessary. Bring to simmering point then cover and cook gently for around 40 minutes. Add the lemon juice and cinnamon and cook for a further 8–10 minutes. Serve warm.

For vine leaves stuffed with puy lentils, replace the lamb with 200 g (7 oz) puy lentils cooked according to the instructions on the packet and use cooked short-grain brown rice. Mix the cooked lentils and rice with the mint, parsley and grated lemon rind and add the mixture to the fried onions, then remove from the heat. Assemble and cook the vine leaves as above.

prawn & coconut balls

Serves **4–6**
Preparation time **15 minutes**
  + 10 minutes resting time
Cooking time **15 minutes**

180 g (6 oz) **long-grain rice**
300 ml (½ pint) **water**
1.5 litres (2½ pints) **coconut milk**
grated rind of 1 **unwaxed lemon**
400 g (13 oz) **raw peeled prawns**
1 teaspoon chopped **fresh root ginger**
1 **egg yolk**
1 slice **plain white bread**, crust removed
1 teaspoon **cornflour**
salt and **pepper**

Prepare the rice. Rinse it several times under cold running water until the water runs clear. Drain it in a sieve and place in a heavy-based saucepan. Pour over the water and add seasoning. Bring to the boil, cover, lower the heat and cook for around 15 minutes.

When the rice is cooked, take the saucepan off the heat and leave to rest, covered, for around 10 minutes. Fluff up the rice with a fork.

Meanwhile, place the coconut milk and lemon rind in a large heavy-based saucepan. Add pepper and bring to simmering point.

Slice the prawns into large pieces and place them in a food-processor along with the ginger, egg yolk, white bread and cornflour. Add a little ground pepper then process well. Shape the mixture into small regular-sized balls, using your fingers. Drop them in the pan of coconut milk and cook at a slow simmer for around 8 minutes.

Drain the prawn balls and serve immediately with the rice.

For curried pork balls, replace the prawns with 400 g (13 oz) minced pork and brown the pork balls in a lightly oiled frying pan, in batches if necessary, before adding them to the coconut milk. When heating the coconut milk, replace the lemon rind and pepper with 3–4 tablespoons of Thai red curry paste.

wok

marinated beef with orange

Serves **4**
Preparation time **20 minutes**
  + 10 minutes resting time
Cooking time **15 minutes**

400 g (13 oz) **beef fillet**
3 tablespoons **soy sauce**
rind of 1 **unwaxed orange**,
  cut into fine strips
180 g (6 oz) **long-grain rice**
300 ml (½ pint) **water**
1 tablespoon **groundnut oil**
3 large **onions**, sliced into
  rounds
salt and **pepper**

Slice the beef fillet into thin strips about 5–6 cm (2–2½ inches) long. Place them in a dish and pour over the soy sauce, mixing well to make sure the beef is fully coated in the soy sauce. Cover closely and leave in the refrigerator while cooking the rice.

Prepare the rice: rinse it several times under cold running water until the water runs clear then drain in a sieve. Place the rice in a heavy-based saucepan. Add the water and seasoning. Bring to the boil, cover, lower the heat and cook for around 15 minutes. Remove the pan from the heat and let stand, covered, for about 10 minutes. Aerate the rice by stirring with chopsticks.

Heat the groundnut oil in a wok. Drop in the drained beef strips and stir-fry over a fairly high heat, then set aside and keep warm on the warming rack of the wok.

Stir-fry the onions in the wok. Add the strips of orange rind. Stir, then add the beef. Season and cook for 1 minute.

Serve immediately, accompanied with plain rice.

For marinated pork with argan oil, slice 400 g (13 oz) pork tenderloin into thin strips about 5–6 cm (2–2½ inches) long and marinate as above. Use the rind of 1 unwaxed lemon instead of the orange, and substitute the groundnut oil with roasted argan oil.

five-spice pork

Serves **4**
Preparation time **20 minutes**
Cooking time **5 minutes**

1 tablespoon **groundnut oil**
½ **red pepper**, sliced into
   thin strips
400 g (13 oz) **pork fillet**,
   cubed
1 teaspoon **five-spice
   powder** or **curry powder**
200 g (7 oz) **cooked long-
   grain rice**
salt and **pepper**

Heat the oil in a wok. Drop in the strips of red pepper and sauté for 1 minute. Add the cubed pork and stir-fry over a high heat for around 2 minutes or until golden. Season and sprinkle with the five-spice or curry powder.

Add the rice to the wok. Reduce the heat and cook for a further 2–3 minutes.

Serve immediately.

For five-spice beef with pak choi, substitute the pork with 400 g (13 oz) cubed beef fillet. Cut the leaves of 1 large head of pak choi into 2 cm (¾ inch) slices and chop the stalks into 1 cm (½ inch) chunks. Stir-fry the pak choi stalks with 200 g (7 oz) trimmed mangetout in ½ tablespoon of oil in a separate wok or saucepan for 2–3 minutes, then add the pak choi leaves and stir-fry until wilted. Cook the beef as above and stir in the pak choi and mangetout just before serving.

prawn & coconut rice

Serves **4**
Preparation time **10 minutes**
  + 10 minutes resting time
Cooking time **15 minutes**

4 tablespoons **groundnut oil**
250 g (8 oz) **Thai fragrant rice**
1 teaspoon **cumin seeds**
1 small **cinnamon stick**
4 **lime leaves**
400 ml (14 fl oz) can **coconut milk**
150 ml (¼ pint) **water**
1 teaspoon **salt**
2 **garlic cloves**, crushed
2.5 cm (1 inch) piece of **fresh root ginger**, peeled and grated
pinch of **crushed dried chillies**
500 g (1 lb) **raw king prawns**, peeled and deveined
2 tablespoons **Thai fish sauce**
1 tablespoon **lime juice**
2 tablespoons chopped **fresh coriander leaves**
25 g (1 oz) **dry-roasted peanuts**, chopped, to garnish

Heat half the oil in a saucepan and stir-fry the rice until all the grains are glossy. Add the cumin seeds, cinnamon stick, lime leaves, coconut milk, water and salt. Bring to the boil and simmer gently over a low heat for 10 minutes. Remove from the heat, cover and leave to rest for 10 minutes.

Meanwhile, heat the remaining oil in a wok and stir-fry the garlic, ginger and crushed dried chillies for 30 seconds. Add the prawns and stir-fry for a further 3–4 minutes, until pink.

Stir in the coconut rice with the fish sauce, lime juice and coriander. Serve scattered with the peanuts.

For coconut & soya bean rice with lime & cherry tomatoes, cook 250 g (8 oz) rice, adding the cumin seeds, cinnamon stick, lime leaves, coconut milk, water and salt as above. Add 175 g (6 oz) soya beans instead of the prawns. Roughly chop a large handful of fresh coriander leaves and halve 175 g (6 oz) cherry tomatoes. Stir them into the rice together with 1 tablespoon of lime juice and the finely grated rind of 1 lime. Stir-fry for 3–4 minutes until hot and cooked through, then serve immediately.

beef with ginger & tomato

Serves **4**
Preparation time **15 minutes**
Cooking time **10 minutes**

400 g (13 oz) **beef fillet**
1 tablespoon **vegetable oil**
1 teaspoon grated **fresh root ginger**
1 teaspoon **tomato concentrate**
pinch of **caster sugar**
2 tablespoons **soy sauce**
400 g (13 oz) **cooked long-grain rice**
salt and **pepper**

Slice the beef fillet into thin strips around 4–5 cm (1½–2 inches) long.

Heat the oil in a wok and add the grated ginger. Turn it in the oil briefly using a wooden spoon, then add the tomato concentrate and the sugar.

Add the beef strips to the wok, stir-fry for 2–3 minutes, then add the soy sauce. Remove the meat, then set aside and keep warm on the warming rack of the wok.

Place the rice in the wok and cook for 2–3 minutes.

Arrange the strips of meat over the rice and serve immediately.

For chicken with tomato & peanut sauce, replace the beef with 400 g (13 oz) sliced chicken breast fillet. Heat the oil as above and add 2 minced garlic cloves with the ginger. Add the tomato concentrate, sugar and chicken, stir-fry for 2–3 minutes, then stir in 2 tablespoons of smooth peanut butter and 2–3 tablespoons of water, omitting the soy sauce. Season with salt to taste, remove from the wok and keep warm while you heat the rice.

lamb meatballs & white rice

Serves **4–6**
Preparation time **25 minutes**
Cooking time **25 minutes**

1 small bunch of **parsley**,
    chopped
600 g (1 ¼ lb) **minced lamb**
2 pinches of **ground
    cinnamon**
2 **eggs**
40 g (1 ½ oz) **pine nuts**
1 tablespoon **flour**
2 tablespoons **vegetable oil**
2 **onions**, finely chopped
800 ml (1 ¼ pints) **vegetable
    stock**
juice of 2 **oranges**
200 g (7 oz) **long-grain rice**
salt and **pepper**

Wash and dry the parsley and chop finely.

Place the lamb in a bowl, sprinkle with the ground cinnamon, season and add the eggs, pine nuts, flour and chopped parsley. Mix well and shape into regular balls, using your hands.

Heat 1 tablespoon of the oil in a wok and stir-fry the onions until they change colour. Add the meatballs, turning with a spatula until golden brown. Cover with 500 ml (17 fl oz) of the stock. Bring to simmering point, then add salt, a little pepper and the orange juice. Cook gently for around 15 minutes.

Meanwhile, heat the remaining oil in a saucepan. Add the rice, turning until translucent. Pour in the remaining stock, add salt and pepper and bring to boiling point. Cover and cook gently for about 15 minutes.

Serve the meatballs with the rice.

For grilled meatballs with yogurt, mix 500 g (1 lb) minced lamb with 125 g (4 oz) stale breadcrumbs, 1 grated onion, 1 crushed garlic clove, 1 egg, 1 tablespoon of chopped parsley and 1 teaspoon of ground cumin. Mix well and shape into regular balls, using your hands. Cook for 7–10 minutes on an oiled tray under a preheated medium-high grill, turning frequently, until golden. Serve with rice and 250 ml (8 oz) yogurt mixed with ¼ cucumber, peeled and diced, 1 crushed garlic clove and 2 teaspoons of finely chopped mint.

small vegetables & black mushrooms

Serves **4**
Preparation time **20 minutes**
+ 30 minutes steeping time
+ 10 minutes resting time
Cooking time **20 minutes**

6 **dried black mushrooms**
200 g (7 oz) **long-grain rice**
300 ml (½ pint) **water**
150 g (5 oz) **fine green
   beans**, washed and trimmed
120 g (4 oz) **broccoli**
1 tablespoon **vegetable oil**
1 **courgette**, sliced into thin
   strips
1 **carrot**, sliced into thin batons
1 teaspoon grated **fresh root
   ginger**
salt and **pepper**

Place the mushrooms in a bowl and cover with warm water. Leave to steep for around 30 minutes.

Place the rice in a heavy-based saucepan. Add the water and season with salt and pepper. Bring to the boil, cover, lower the heat and cook for around 15 minutes. Take the pan off the heat and stand, covered, for about 10 minutes. Fluff up the rice by stirring it with chopsticks.

Meanwhile, cut the green beans into 4 cm (1½ inch) slices. Break the broccoli into florets. Rinse and drain them. Drain the mushrooms well, remove the stalks and slice the caps finely.

Heat the oil in a wok. Stir-fry all the vegetables for 3–4 minutes. Season with salt and pepper, then sprinkle with the grated ginger. Serve with the hot rice.

For chunky vegetables with chickpeas, replace the black mushrooms with 200 g (7 oz) fresh chestnut mushrooms, cut into quarters. Slice the courgette and carrot into diagonal slices. Stir-fry the grated ginger in the oil in the wok then add the vegetables and stir-fry for 3 minutes. Add 400 g (13 oz) canned chickpeas, drained and stir-fry for a further 2 minutes.

pilaf with saffron & chicken

Serves **4**
Preparation time **15 minutes**
Cooking time **35 minutes**

1 ½ teaspoons **ground saffron**
300 ml (½ pint) **water**
1 tablespoon **vegetable oil**
4 **garlic cloves**, finely chopped
4 **shallots**, chopped
1 teaspoon grated **fresh root ginger**
200 g (7 oz) **basmati rice**
2 pinches of **paprika powder**
200 g (7 oz) **pork fillet**, cubed
200 g (7 oz) **chicken breast**, diced
salt and **pepper**

Dissolve the saffron in the water and heat gently in a saucepan.

Heat the oil in a wok. Add the garlic, shallots and grated ginger. Cook for 2 minutes, then add the rice. Turn in the oil until it becomes translucent. Add the saffron-flavoured water, season and sprinkle with paprika. Bring to simmering point, cover and leave simmering for 15–20 minutes.

Meanwhile, cook the cubed pork and diced chicken in a lightly oiled saucepan until they are golden.

Serve the rice topped with the cooked meat.

For tofu & mushroom pilaf rice, replace the pork fillet and chicken breast with 200 g (7 oz) tofu, cut into 2 cm (¾ inch) cubes, and 200 g (7 oz) shiitake mushrooms. Cook the tofu cubes in a lightly oiled saucepan until golden, then add the shiitake mushroom and stir-fry for a further 2–3 minutes. Add 1 tablespoon of light soy sauce before serving.

carrots, bean sprouts & mangetout

Serves **4**
Preparation time **15 minutes**
  + 10 minutes resting time
Cooking time **15 minutes**

200 g (7 oz) **long-grain rice**
350 ml (12 fl oz) **water**
200 g (7 oz) **mangetout**
2 **carrots**
120 g (4 oz) **bean sprouts**
1 **garlic clove**
1 tablespoon **vegetable oil**
1 teaspoon grated **fresh root ginger**
3 teaspoons **soy sauce**
pinch of **caster sugar**
80 ml (3 fl oz) **warm water**
salt and **pepper**

Place the rice in a heavy-based saucepan. Add the water and season to taste. Bring to the boil, then cover. Lower the heat and cook for around 15 minutes. Take the pan off the heat and leave it resting, covered, for about 10 minutes. Aerate the rice by stirring it with chopsticks.

Top and tail the mangetout, removing any stringy bits. Rinse and drain, then cut them in half. Peel and grate the carrots. Pick over the bean sprouts, wash them in cold water and drain. Peel and finely chop the garlic.

Heat the oil in a wok. Quickly stir-fry the garlic and ginger then add the mangetout, carrots and bean sprouts. Stir-fry for 2–3 minutes then add the soy sauce, caster sugar and warm water. Cover and leave to simmer for 3 minutes.

Serve the vegetables with the hot rice.

For vegetable stir-fry with nuts & seeds, coat 75 g (3 oz) cashew nuts and 25 g (1 oz) sunflower seeds in 1 teaspoon of tamari sauce (Japanese soy sauce) and toast under a medium-hot grill for 4–5 minutes, until golden. Serve sprinkled over the vegetables.

basic cantonese rice

Serves **4**
Preparation time **10 minutes**
Cooking time **15 minutes**

100 g (3½ oz) fresh shelled
  baby peas
2 **eggs**, well beaten
2 thick slices **cooked ham**
1 tablespoon **vegetable oil**
180 g (6 oz) **cooked long-
  grain rice**
2 teaspoons **soy sauce**
salt and **pepper**

Place the peas in a saucepan of boiling salted water
and cook for about 5 minutes. Drain and run under
cold water.

Lightly salt the beaten eggs and cook as for an
omelette. Remove from the pan with the aid of a
wooden spatula, then slice into thin strips.

Dice the ham slices finely.

Heat the oil in a wok, add the rice and cook for
2 minutes. Add the peas, the diced ham and the
omelette strips. Pour over the soy sauce, season,
stir well and serve.

For Cantonese rice with chicken & shrimps, stir-fry
125 g (4 oz) diced chicken breast with 2 crushed garlic
cloves for 3 minutes then add 125 g (4 oz) peeled
cooked shrimps and cook for a further 1 minute. Add
the remaining ingredients as above.

chinese fried rice with shrimps

Serves **4**
Preparation time **10 minutes**
  + 15 minutes steeping time
Cooking time **15 minutes**

80 g (3 oz) **dried shrimps**
2 **eggs**, well beaten
100 g (3½ oz) fresh shelled
  baby peas
2 **spring onions**
1 **shallot**
125 g (4 oz) **roast pork**
1 tablespoon **vegetable oil**
180 g (6 oz) **cooked long-
  grain rice**
2 teaspoons **soy sauce**
salt and **pepper**

Place the shrimps in a bowl, cover with warm water and leave to steep for 15 minutes.

Make an omelette with the eggs then cut into thin strips. Cook the peas in boiling water for 5 minutes.

Wash the spring onions and slice into small pieces. Peel and finely chop the shallot. Cut the roast pork into small dice. Peel the shrimps if unpeeled.

Heat the oil in a wok and cook the chopped shallot until it changes colour. Add the cooked rice and heat for 2 minutes. Add the shrimps, diced pork, omelette strips, spring onions and peas. Sprinkle with soy sauce, season, stir and serve.

For Chinese fried rice with lardons, omit the shrimps and roast pork. Cook the chopped shallot as above, adding ½ red chilli, finely chopped, and 1 tablespoon of grated fresh root ginger to the oil, then add 125 g (4 oz) bacon lardons to the wok and cook for a further 2 minutes. Complete the recipe as above.

chinese fried rice with red pepper

Serves **4**
Preparation time **10 minutes**
Cooking time **15 minutes**

2 **eggs**, well beaten
100 g (3½ oz) fresh shelled
  baby peas
1 tablespoon **vegetable oil**
2 **onions**, chopped
1 **shallot**, chopped
½ **red pepper**, finely diced
125 g (4 oz) **cooked long-**
  grain rice
100 g (3½ oz) **fresh peeled**
  cooked shrimps
2 teaspoons **soy sauce**
salt and **pepper**

Make an omelette with the eggs then slice into thin strips. Cook the peas for 5 minutes in boiling water, then drain.

Heat the vegetable oil in a wok. Add the onions and shallot and cook for a few minutes until they change colour. Add the diced red pepper and cook for a further minute. Stir in the rice and heat for 2 minutes.

Add the shrimps, peas and omelette strips. Pour over the soy sauce, season, stir and serve.

For Chinese fried rice with tofu, omit the eggs and shrimps. Stir-fry 200 g (7 oz) cubed tofu in 1 tablespoon of vegetable oil, flavoured with 1 crushed garlic clove and 1 teaspoon of grated fresh root ginger, until golden, then remove from the wok and drain on kitchen paper. Fry the onions and shallot as above, adding more vegetable oil to the wok if necessary. Add the diced red pepper and continue as above, returning the tofu to the wok with the peas.

chinese fried rice with sausage

Serves **4**
Preparation time **10 minutes**
Cooking time **15 minutes**

100 g (3½ oz) **broccoli**
100 g (3½ oz) fresh shelled
  baby peas
2 **eggs**, well beaten
2 **smoked sausages**
2 **spring onions**
1 tablespoon **vegetable oil**
120 g (3½ oz) **cooked
  long-grain rice**
2 teaspoons **soy sauce**
salt and **pepper**

Wash the broccoli, drain and cut into small florets. Cook for 4 minutes in a saucepan of boiling salted water, then rinse under cold running water and drain well. Cook the peas for 5 minutes in boiling water.

Make an omelette with the eggs and slice it thinly. Cut the sausages into rounds. Wash and dry the spring onions and chop finely.

Heat the oil in a wok, add the rice and let it warm up for 2 minutes. Add the sliced sausage, egg strips, broccoli, peas and spring onions. Pour over the soy sauce, season, stir and serve.

For fried wild rice with smoked sausage & chicken, substitute the long-grain rice with 120 g (3½ oz) cooked wild rice. Omit the eggs and add 175 g (6 oz) shredded smoked chicken with the sausage and vegetables. Add a few drops of toasted sesame oil before serving.

nasi goreng

Serves **4**
Preparation time **10 minutes**
Cooking time **10 minutes**

2 tablespoons **vegetable oil**
150 g (5 oz) **boneless,
skinless chicken breast**,
finely chopped
50 g (2 oz) **cooked peeled
shrimps**, defrosted if frozen
1 **garlic clove**, crushed
1 **carrot**, grated
¼ **white cabbage**, thinly
sliced
1 **egg**, beaten
300 g (10 oz) cold **cooked
basmati rice**
2 tablespoons **kecap manis**
(sweet soy sauce)
½ teaspoon **sesame oil**
1 tablespoon **chilli sauce**
1 **red chilli**, deseeded and cut
into strips, to garnish

Heat the oil in a wok or large frying pan, add the chicken
and stir-fry for 1 minute. Add the shrimps, garlic, carrot
and cabbage and stir-fry for 3–4 minutes.

Pour in the egg and spread it out using a wooden spoon.
Cook until set, then add the rice and break up the egg,
stirring it in.

Add the kecap manis, sesame oil and chilli sauce and
heat through. Serve immediately, garnished with the chilli
strips.

For vegetarian nasi goreng, crush a garlic clove and
stir-fry it in 2 tablespoons of oil with 1 chopped carrot
and ¼ chopped white cabbage. Omit the chicken and
shrimps but add 1 finely sliced red pepper, 125 g (4 oz)
sliced shiitake mushrooms and 2 heads finely shredded
pak choi. Stir-fry for a further 2–3 minutes until the
vegetables are soft yet still retaining their shape. Add the
remaining ingredients and serve in warm serving bowls.

takes time

parmesan risotto

Serves **4**
Preparation time **5 minutes**
Cooking time **25 minutes**

1 litre (1¾ pints) **chicken stock**
2 tablespoons **olive oil**
2 **shallots**, finely chopped
200 g (7 oz) **'superfino' risotto rice**
50 ml (2 fl oz) **dry white wine**
20 g (¾ oz) **butter**, diced
40 g (1½ oz) **Parmesan cheese**, freshly grated
finely chopped **parsley**, to garnish

Heat the chicken stock gently in a saucepan.

Heat the olive oil in a heavy-based saucepan. Add the shallots and cook gently for 2 minutes until they change colour. Add the rice and turn with a spatula for a few minutes until the grains are coated with the oil. Add the white wine and keep stirring.

Add a small ladleful of chicken stock to the pan, allow the rice to absorb the liquid, then add another ladleful of stock. Continue adding the remaining hot stock little by little, each time waiting until the last spoonful has been fully absorbed.

Take the pan of rice off the heat and add the diced butter and grated Parmesan. Let it stand briefly before mixing in. The rice should take on a creamy consistency. Sprinkle with chopped parsley and serve immediately.

For red risotto, replace the chicken stock with 1 litre (1¾ pints) vegetable stock. Replace the risotto rice with 200 g (7 oz) Camargue red rice and cook as above. To serve, drizzle with parsley oil made from 50 ml (2 fl oz) extra virgin olive oil blended with ¼ teaspoon of sherry vinegar, 2 tablespoons of finely chopped parsley, 1 minced garlic clove and seasoning to taste.

146

saffron risotto with ceps

Serves **4**
Preparation time **5 minutes**
Cooking time **25 minutes**

1 litre (1¾ pints) **chicken stock**
4 **saffron threads**
300 g (10 oz) **fresh ceps**
40 g (1½ oz) **butter**
1 **onion**, finely chopped
4 tablespoons finely chopped **parsley**
200 g (7 oz) **'superfino' risotto rice**
50 ml (2 fl oz) **dry white wine**
40 g (1½ oz) **Parmesan cheese**, freshly grated

Gently heat the chicken stock in a saucepan. Add the saffron threads, cover the pan and leave to infuse. Clean the ceps, remove the stalks and dice roughly.

Melt 20 g (¾ oz) butter in a nonstick saucepan and add the chopped onion. Cook until it turns golden then add the ceps. Sauté briefly then add the chopped parsley. Set aside and keep warm.

Melt the remaining butter in a heavy-based saucepan. Add the rice. Dampen with the wine and let the grains absorb the liquid. Remove the saffron from the stock.

Add a small ladleful of chicken stock to the pan, allow the rice to absorb the liquid, then add another ladleful of stock. Continue adding the remaining hot stock little by little, each time waiting until the last spoonful has been fully absorbed.

Remove the pan of rice from the heat and add the grated Parmesan. Let stand for a moment before mixing in. The rice will take on a creamy consistency. Add the diced ceps and blend in well. Serve immediately.

For risotto with shiitake mushrooms, replace the ceps with 300 g (10 oz) thinly sliced shiitake mushrooms. Do not use saffron but add ½ teaspoon of smoked sweet paprika to the pan when cooking the onions.

pea & prawn risotto

Serves **6**
Preparation time **10 minutes**
Cooking time **40 minutes**

500 g (1 lb) **raw prawns in their shells**
125 g (4 oz) **butter**
1 **onion**, finely chopped
2 **garlic cloves**, crushed
250 g (8 oz) **risotto rice**
375 g (12 oz) **fresh peas**
150 ml (¼ pint) **dry white wine**
1.5 litres (2½ pints) **hot vegetable stock**
4 tablespoons chopped **mint**

Peel the prawns, reserving the heads and shells. Melt 100 g (3½ oz) butter in a large frying pan and fry the prawn heads and shells for 3–4 minutes. Strain and return butter to the pan, discarding heads and shells.

Add the onion and garlic and cook for 5 minutes until softened but not coloured. Add the rice and stir well to coat the grains with the butter. Add the peas, then pour in the wine. Bring to the boil and cook, stirring, until reduced by half.

Add the hot stock, a large ladleful at a time, and cook, stirring constantly until each addition has been absorbed before adding the next. Continue in this way until all the stock has been absorbed and the rice is creamy but the grains are still firm. This should take about 20 minutes.

Melt the remaining butter in a separate frying pan, add the prawns and cook, stirring, for 3–4 minutes. Stir into the rice with the pan juices and mint, and season to taste with salt and pepper.

For pea & prawn risotto cakes, cook the risotto as above, then cool. Stir in 2 beaten eggs and 50 g (2 oz) grated Parmesan cheese. Using damp hands, shape the mixture into 10 cm (4 inch) patties. Heat a shallow depth of vegetable oil in a frying pan; cook the cakes, in batches, for 3–4 minutes on each side until golden brown and heated through. Remove from the pan with a slotted spoon and keep warm while you cook the remainder. Serve with a crisp green salad.

risotto nero

Serves **4**
Preparation time **5 minutes**
Cooking time **1 hour**

1 litre (1¾ pints) **chicken stock**
2 tablespoons **olive oil**
200 g (7 oz) **riso venere nero integrale** (black venus rice)
20 g (¾ oz) **butter**, diced
40 g (1½ oz) **Parmesan cheese**, freshly grated

Place the chicken stock in a saucepan and heat gently.

Heat the olive oil in a heavy-based saucepan. Add the rice, brown for a few seconds and stir with a spatula to ensure the grains are coated with the oil.

Add a small ladleful of chicken stock to the pan, allow the rice to absorb the liquid, then add another ladleful of stock. Continue adding the remaining hot stock little by little, each time waiting until the last spoonful has been fully absorbed.

Remove the pan of rice from the heat. Add the diced butter and the grated Parmesan. Let it rest briefly before mixing in. The rice will take on a creamy consistency. Serve hot.

For black risotto primavera, trim 200 g (7 oz) asparagus, cut each spear diagonally into four and cook in unsalted boiling water for 3–4 minutes, depending on the thickness. Drain and pat dry with kitchen paper. Cook 125 g (4 oz) shelled baby broad beans in unsalted boiling water for 4 minutes, adding 125 g (4 oz) shelled baby peas after 2 minutes. Drain the broad beans and peas, plunge them immediately into iced water, and drain again. Cook the risotto as above, using 1 litre (1¾ pints) vegetable stock instead of the chicken stock. Add the vegetables to the risotto just before it is cooked to heat through.

crayfish risotto

Serves **4**
Preparation time **10 minutes**
Cooking time **30 minutes**

50 g (2 oz) **butter**
2 **shallots**, finely chopped
1 **mild red chilli**, thinly sliced
1 teaspoon **mild paprika**
1 **garlic clove**, crushed
300 g (10 oz) **risotto rice**
1 glass **dry white wine**, about
    150 ml (¼ pint)
a few **lemon thyme sprigs**
about 1.2 litres (2 pints) **hot
    fish stock** or **chicken
    stock**
3 tablespoons roughly
    chopped **fresh tarragon**
300 g (10 oz) **crayfish tails
    in brine**, drained
salt
freshly grated **Parmesan
    cheese**, to garnish

Melt half the butter in a large saucepan or deep-sided sauté pan and gently fry the shallots until softened. Add the chilli, paprika and garlic and fry gently for 30 seconds, without browning the garlic.

Sprinkle in the rice and fry gently for 1 minute, stirring. Add the wine and let it bubble until almost evaporated.

Add the thyme and a ladleful of the stock and cook, stirring, until the rice has almost absorbed the stock. Continue cooking, adding the stock a ladleful at a time, and letting the rice absorb most of the stock before adding more. Once the rice is tender but retaining a little bite, the risotto is ready – this will take about 25 minutes. You may not need all the stock.

Stir in the tarragon, crayfish and remaining butter and heat through gently for 1 minute. Add a little extra salt if necessary and serve immediately, garnished with Parmesan and with a watercress salad, if you like.

For prawn risotto, cook 350 g (11½ oz) raw peeled prawns in the butter, as in the first step. Cook until pink, drain, then return to the pan in the fourth step. Omit the chilli and replace the shallots with 1 bunch of chopped spring onions.

green risotto

Serves **4**
Preparation time **10 minutes**
Cooking time **30 minutes**

125 g (4 oz) **butter**
1 tablespoon **olive oil**
1 **garlic clove**, crushed or
    chopped
1 **onion**, finely diced
300 g (10 oz) **risotto rice**
1 litre (1¾ pints) **hot
    vegetable stock**
125 g (4 oz) **green beans**, cut
    into short lengths
125 g (4 oz) fresh shelled
    peas
125 g (4 oz) **broad beans**
125 g (4 oz) **asparagus**, cut
    into short lengths
125 g (4 oz) **baby spinach**,
    chopped
75 ml (3 fl oz) **dry vermouth**
    or **white wine**
2 tablespoons chopped
    parsley
125 g (4 oz) **Parmesan
    cheese**, freshly grated
salt and **pepper**

Melt half the butter with the oil in a large saucepan, add the garlic and onion and fry gently for 5 minutes.

Add the rice and stir well to coat each grain with the butter and oil. Add enough stock to just cover the rice and stir well. Simmer gently, stirring frequently, until most of the liquid is absorbed.

Pour in more stock and stir well. Continue adding the stock a little at a time, stirring until it is absorbed and the rice is tender but retaining a little bite – this will take about 25 minutes. You may not need all the stock. About 5 minutes before the end of the cooking time, add the vegetables and vermouth or wine and mix well.

Remove the pan from the heat, season and add the remaining butter, the parsley and the Parmesan cheese. Mix well and serve.

For saffron & tomato risotto, omit the peas, asparagus and spinach from the above recipe. Add 75 g (3 oz) pine nuts to the pan when melting the butter. Fry until golden, then drain before adding the garlic and onions. Crumble in 1 teaspoon of saffron threads with the rice. Add 300 g (10 oz) halved cherry tomatoes at the end of the third step, cooking for 2–3 minutes until heated through, then stir in the pine nuts and a handful of shredded basil leaves.

butternut squash risotto

Serves **4**
Preparation time **15 minutes**
Cooking time **30 minutes**

2 tablespoons **olive oil**
1 **onion**, finely chopped
500 g (1 lb) **butternut
  squash**, peeled, deseeded
  and roughly chopped
250 g (8 oz) **risotto rice**
900 ml (1 ½ pints) **rich
  chicken stock**
75 g (3 oz) **Parmesan
  cheese**, freshly grated, plus
  extra to serve
4 tablespoons **pine nuts**,
  toasted
250 g (8 oz) **fresh spinach
  leaves**

Heat the oil in a large heavy-based frying pan and cook
the onion and squash over a low to moderate heat for
10 minutes until softened.

Add the rice and cook for 1 minute, then add half the
stock. Bring to the boil, then reduce the heat and simmer
gently for 5 minutes until almost all the stock has been
absorbed, stirring occasionally.

Continue to add the stock 150 ml (¼ pint) at a time
and cook over a gentle heat until almost all the stock
has been absorbed before adding more. Once the rice is
tender, remove the pan from the heat, add the Parmesan,
pine nuts and spinach and stir well to combine and
wilt the spinach, returning to the heat for 1 minute if
necessary.

Serve in warmed serving bowls with extra freshly grated
Parmesan.

For chicken & pea risotto, replace the butternut
squash with 3 x 150 g (5 oz) chicken breasts, chopped
and cooked with the onion. Cook in the same way as
above, adding an additional 125 g (4 oz) frozen peas and
adding the spinach if liked. Serve with extra Parmesan
sprinkled over.

beetroot risotto

Serves **4**
Preparation time
5–10 minutes
Cooking time **30 minutes**

1 tablespoon **olive oil**
15 g (½ oz) **butter**
1 teaspoon crushed or coarsely
  ground **coriander seeds**
4 **spring onions**, thinly sliced
400 g (13 oz) freshly cooked
  beetroot, cut into 1 cm
  (½ inch) dice
500 g (1 lb) **risotto rice**
1.5 litres (2½ pints) **hot
  vegetable stock**
200 g (7 oz) **cream cheese**
4 tablespoons finely chopped
  dill
salt and **pepper**
dill sprigs and **crème
  fraîche**, to garnish

Heat the oil and butter in a large saucepan. Add the crushed or ground coriander seeds and spring onions and stir-fry briskly for 1 minute.

Add the beetroot and the rice. Cook, stirring, for 2–3 minutes to coat all the grains with oil and butter. Gradually pour in the hot stock a ladleful at a time, stirring frequently until each ladleful is absorbed before adding the next. This should take about 25 minutes, by which time the rice should be tender, but retaining a little bite.

Stir in the cream cheese and dill and season to taste. Serve immediately, garnished with dill sprigs and a little crème fraîche, if using.

For spinach & lemon risotto, heat the oil and butter and cook 2 finely chopped shallots and 2 crushed garlic cloves for 3 minutes. Stir in 300 g (10 oz) risotto rice and gradually add 1 litre (1¾ pints) vegetable stock as above. Before you add the last of the stock, stir in 500 g (1 lb) chopped spinach, the grated rind and juice of 1 lemon and season. Increase the heat and stir, then add the remaining stock and 50 g (2 oz) butter and cook for a few minutes. Stir in 50 g (2 oz) grated Parmesan. Garnish with more Parmesan, and grated lemon rind, if you like, before serving.

parma ham & sweet potato risotto

Serves **4**
Preparation time **5 minutes**
Cooking time **25 minutes**

2 medium **sweet potatoes**,
   scrubbed and cut into
   1 cm (½ inch) chunks
50 g (2 oz) **butter**
1 bunch of **spring onions**,
   finely sliced
375 g (12 oz) **risotto rice**
2 **bay leaves**
1.2 litres (2 pints) **hot
   chicken stock** or
   vegetable stock
3 tablespoons **olive oil**
75 g (3 oz) **Parma ham**,
   torn into pieces
25 g (1 oz) **mixed fresh
   herbs**, such as parsley,
   chervil, tarragon and chives,
   chopped
salt and **pepper**

Cook the sweet potatoes in lightly salted boiling water for 2–3 minutes to soften. Drain and set aside.

Meanwhile, melt the butter in a large, heavy-based saucepan. Add the spring onions and sauté for 1 minute. Add the rice and stir well to coat the grains with the butter.

Add the bay leaves to the rice. Add the hot stock, a large ladleful at a time, stirring until each addition is absorbed into the rice. Continue adding stock in this way, cooking until the rice is creamy but the grains are still firm. This should take about 20 minutes.

Meanwhile, heat 1 tablespoon of the oil in a frying pan and cook the ham until golden. Drain and keep warm. Add the remaining oil and fry the sweet potatoes, turning frequently, for 6–8 minutes, until golden.

Add the herbs to the risotto and season to taste with salt and pepper, then add the ham and sweet potatoes, folding in gently. Cover and leave the risotto to rest for a few minutes before serving.

For roasted tomato, Parma ham & brie risotto, halve 8 plum tomatoes, season and drizzle with 3 tablespoons of olive oil. Roast in a preheated oven, 200°C (400°F), Gas Mark 6, for 30 minutes until lightly charred and soft. Let cool. Cook the risotto as above, stirring in the roasted tomato and 125 g (4 oz) creamy brie cubes at the end of the cooking instead of the sweet potatoes. Season generously.

biryani

Serves **4**
Preparation time **25 minutes**
Cooking time **40 minutes**

3 **onions**
2 **garlic cloves**, chopped
25 g (1 oz) **fresh root ginger**,
 roughly chopped
2 teaspoons **ground turmeric**
¼ teaspoon **ground cloves**
½ teaspoon **dried chilli
 flakes**
¼ teaspoon **ground
 cinnamon**
2 teaspoons **medium curry
 paste**
1 tablespoon **lemon juice**
2 teaspoons **caster sugar**
300 g (10 oz) **lean chicken,
 turkey breast** or **lamb
 fillet**, cut into small pieces
6 tablespoons **vegetable oil**
1 small **cauliflower**, cut into
 small florets
2 **bay leaves**
300 g (10 oz) **basmati rice**
750 ml (1¼ pints) **chicken
 stock** or **vegetable stock**
1 tablespoon **black onion
 seeds**
salt and **pepper**
2 tablespoons toasted
 flaked almonds, to garnish

Chop 1 onion and put in a food processor with the garlic, ginger, turmeric, cloves, chilli flakes, cinnamon, curry paste, lemon juice, sugar and salt and pepper. Blend to a thick paste and turn into a bowl. Add the meat to the bowl and mix together well.

Slice the second onion thinly. Heat 5 tablespoons of the oil in a large frying pan and fry the onion slices until deep golden and crisp. Drain on kitchen paper.

Add the cauliflower to the frying pan and fry gently for 5 minutes. Chop the third onion, add it to the pan and fry gently, stirring, for a further 5 minutes until the cauliflower is softened and golden. Drain. Heat the remaining oil in the pan. Tip in the meat and marinade and fry gently for 5 minutes, stirring.

Stir in the bay leaves, rice and stock and bring to the boil. Reduce the heat and simmer very gently, stirring occasionally, for 10–12 minutes until the rice is tender and the stock absorbed, adding a little water to the pan if the mixture is dry before the rice is cooked. Stir in the black onion seeds. Return the cauliflower mixture to the pan and heat through. Serve scattered with the crisp onion and toasted almonds accompanied by a cucumber raita (see below), if you like.

For cucumber & mint raita, gently mix together 175 g (6 oz) natural yogurt, 75 g (3 oz) cucumber, deseeded and coarsely grated, 2 tablespoons of chopped mint, 1 pinch of ground cumin and lemon juice and salt to taste. Stand for 30 minutes.

minestrone with mint

Serves **4**
Preparation time **10 minutes**
Cooking time **30 minutes**

150 g (5 oz) **fine green beans**
1 **celery stick**
1 tablespoon **olive oil**
½ **red pepper**, finely diced
2 **carrots**, sliced into thin rounds
1 litre (1¾ pints) **water**
80 g (3 oz) **risotto rice**
100 g (3½ oz) fresh shelled **baby peas**
2 tablespoons finely chopped **mint leaves**
80 g (3 oz) **Parmesan cheese**, grated
salt and **pepper**

Top and tail the fine green beans. Wash them and cut into slices around 5 cm (2 inches) long. Wash the celery stick and cut into small rounds.

Heat the oil in a saucepan and lightly brown the beans, celery, pepper and carrots for a few moments, stirring. Season.

Add the water, bring to the boil and add the rice and peas. Cover tightly and leave simmering for around 25 minutes.

Add the chopped mint leaves 5 minutes before the end of cooking. Grind in some pepper and sprinkle with grated Parmesan just before serving.

For rice & bean soup, omit the fine green beans, red pepper, carrots and peas. Fry 1 small fennel bulb, trimmed and finely chopped, with the celery. Add 1 litre (1¾ pints) vegetable stock instead of the water, then add the rice, 400 g (13 oz) canned chopped tomatoes, drained, and 400 g (13 oz) canned cannellini beans, drained. Replace the mint with 2 tablespoons of chopped parsley.

coriander lentils

Serves **4**
Preparation time **10 minutes**
Cooking time **30 minutes**

600 ml (1 pint) **chicken stock**
1 tablespoon **vegetable oil**
2 **onions**, finely chopped
100 g (3½ oz) **basmati rice**
100 g (3½ oz) **red lentils**
2 teaspoons **cumin seeds**
1 **clove**
1 small **cinnamon stick**
2 tablespoons **coriander leaves**
salt and **pepper**

Place the chicken stock in a saucepan and bring to simmering point.

Heat the oil in a saucepan and cook the onions gently until golden, then remove half the fried onions from the pan and set aside.

Add the rice and lentils to the pan and stir with a spoon. Add the chicken stock. Add the cumin seeds, clove and cinnamon stick. Cover and cook over a low heat for around 25 minutes, then remove from the heat and leave to cool.

Sprinkle with the reserved fried onions and coriander leaves just before serving.

For lamb & coconut meatballs, to serve as an accompaniment, make little meatballs using 300 g (10 oz) of chopped mutton or lamb, 1 bunch of coriander, finely chopped, 1 egg, 100 ml (3½ fl oz) coconut milk and 2 pinches of strong curry powder. Chill the meatballs for 1 hour in the refrigerator, then deep-fry for 5 minutes. Drain carefully on kitchen paper and serve hot with the coriander lentils.

gazpacho

Serves **4**

Preparation time **20 minutes**
  + 1½ hours resting time

3 **garlic cloves**
5 tablespoons **olive oil**
500 g (1 lb) **ripe tomatoes**
1 small **cucumber**
1 **yellow pepper**, diced into
  small pieces
1 **onion**, finely chopped
3 tablespoons **aged wine
  vinegar**
4 tablespoons **cooked
  partially polished rice**
dash of **Tabasco**
salt and **pepper**

Peel the garlic cloves, remove the germ, and crush the cloves in a mortar with a pinch of salt. Blend in the olive oil, then set aside for 20 minutes.

Plunge the tomatoes in a saucepan of boiling water for 1 minute. Remove the skin and dice the flesh.

Rinse the cucumber, then peel and dice it.

Place the tomatoes, cucumber, yellow pepper and onion in a food-processor, add the vinegar and the oil with the garlic, then process thoroughly. Stir in the cooked rice, add salt and pepper and chill in the refrigerator for at least 1½ hours. Add a dash of Tabasco sauce and serve cold.

For chilled spinach soup, steam 500 g (1 lb) washed and drained spinach until wilted. Using a hand-held blender, purée the spinach with 250 ml (8 fl oz) vegetable stock. Stir in 500 g (8 oz) natural yogurt, 2 finely chopped spring onions and a generous pinch of cumin. Stir in 4 tablespoons of cooked partially polished rice, add salt and pepper and chill in the refrigerator for at least 1½ hours. Serve cold.

stuffed courgettes

Serves **4–6**
Preparation time **25 minutes**
Cooking time **30 minutes**

1 **onion**, finely chopped
1 tablespoon **olive oil**
1 **thyme sprig**
8–10 small round
   courgettes
60 g (2½ oz) **cooked ham**,
   chopped
1 **garlic clove**, chopped
60 g (2½ oz) **cooked
   long-grain rice**
80 g (3 oz) **Parmesan
   cheese**, grated
7 **basil leaves**, chopped
2 **eggs**
salt and **pepper**

Cook the onion gently with the olive oil and thyme in a saucepan for 5 minutes.

Blanch the courgettes for 5 minutes in a large saucepan of boiling water. Drain, then cut them in two from top to bottom and scoop out the flesh with a small spoon.

Mash the courgette flesh with a fork while mixing it with the onion, ham, garlic, rice, Parmesan, basil leaves and eggs. Season to taste.

Fill the courgette halves with the stuffing. Place them in a gratin dish and cook in a preheated oven, 180°C (350°F), Gas Mark 4, for 25 minutes.

For hazelnut-stuffed courgettes, use 4–6 large courgettes, halved lengthways. Scoop out and discard the seeds. Cook the onion and thyme in olive oil as above, then mix with 1 minced garlic clove, 60 g (2½ oz) cooked long-grain rice, 100 g (3½ oz) finely chopped roasted hazelnuts, 50 g (2 oz) of grated Parmesan, 2 finely chopped sage leaves and 1 beaten egg. Season to taste. Fill the courgette halves with the mixture, top with thin slices of tomato, and sprinkle with 25 (1 oz) grated Parmesan. Cook as above.

stuffed aubergines

Serves **4**
Preparation time **30 minutes**
Cooking time **25 minutes**

4 **aubergines**
300 g (10 oz) **minced lamb**
2 pinches of **ground cinnamon**
1 tablespoon **olive oil**
1 **onion**, chopped
80 g (3 oz) **cooked long-grain rice**
20 g (¾ oz) **pine nuts**
2 tablespoons finely chopped **mint leaves**
2 tablespoons finely chopped **parsley**
salt and **pepper**

Rinse and dry the aubergines, then cut them in two lengthways and hollow out some of the flesh with a small spoon. Place the shells in a baking dish in a preheated oven, 180°C (350°F), Gas Mark 5, for around 10 minutes.

Season the minced lamb with the cinnamon, salt and pepper.

Heat the olive oil in a nonstick saucepan. Cook the chopped onion until golden, then add the lamb, rice, pine nuts, mint and chopped parsley and mix well.

Fill the aubergines with this mixture and return to the oven for around 15 minutes. If necessary, add a little water in the bottom of the dish to make sure they do not stick. Serve warm or cold.

For stuffed aubergines with beans, use 80 g (3 oz) cooked brown rice and replace the lamb with 400 g (13 oz) canned borlotti beans, drained and roughly crushed. Add 125 g (4 oz) sliced chestnut mushrooms to the cooked onion and fry briefly before adding the remaining ingredients.

stuffed tomatoes

Serves **4–6**
Preparation time **25 minutes**
Cooking time **40 minutes**

6 large **tomatoes**
200 g (7 oz) **baby button mushrooms**, finely sliced
1 tablespoon **olive oil**
3 tablespoons finely chopped **parsley**
60 g (2½ oz) **cooked long-grain rice**
2 **eggs**
40 g (1½ oz) **Comté cheese**, grated
2 tablespoons finely chopped **basil**
1 **garlic clove**, chopped
salt and **pepper**

Wash and dry the tomatoes, cut off the tops and scoop out the seeds.

Cook the mushrooms gently in a saucepan with the olive oil. Season them, add the chopped parsley, then remove from the heat.

Mix together the mushrooms and parsley with the rice, eggs, cheese, basil and garlic. Season to taste. Stuff the tomatoes with this mixture then place on an oiled roasting pan in a preheated oven, 180°C (350°F), Gas Mark 4, for around 30 minutes.

For chestnut-stuffed mushrooms, make the stuffing mixture as above, replacing the Comté cheese with 40 g (1½ oz) crumbled Stilton cheese and the basil with 1 tablespoon of finely chopped sage. Add 100 g (3½ oz) chopped roasted chestnuts to the stuffing mixture. Divide the mixture between 4–6 large portobello mushrooms and cook as above.

stuffed peppers

Serves **4–6**
Preparation time **20 minutes**
Cooking time **55 minutes**

150 ml (¼ pint) **water**
60 g (2½ oz) **long-grain rice**
4 **red peppers**
1 **onion**
1 tablespoon **olive oil**
200 g (7 oz) **minced lamb**
20 g (¾ oz) **pine nuts**
20 g (¾ oz) **raisins**
2 **eggs**
salt and **pepper**

Bring the water to the boil in a large saucepan. Add salt, pour in the rice and stir. Cover and lower the heat. Cook for around 12 minutes. The rice should be cooked but still retain some bite. Drain well.

Meanwhile, wash and dry the peppers, cut them in half lengthways and remove the seeds.

Peel and slice the onion. Fry gently in a saucepan with the olive oil. Add the minced lamb, season and mix well. Cook over a low heat. Remove from the heat and set aside to cool.

Dry-fry the pine nuts lightly in a saucepan.

Mix together the rice, onion, lamb, pine nuts, raisins and eggs. Fill the half-peppers with this stuffing then place them in an ovenproof dish. Add 2 tablespoons of water to the bottom of the dish and place in a preheated oven, 180°C (350°F), Gas Mark 4, for 35 minutes.

For stuffed peppers with feta, replace the lamb with 200 g (7 oz) cubed feta cheese and the raisins with 6 green olives, roughly chopped. Add the grated rind of 1 lemon and 2 teaspoons of finely chopped mint to the stuffing mixture.

gratin of rice, yogurt sauce & chilli

Serves **4–6**
Preparation time **20 minutes**
Cooking time **55 minutes**

600 g (1¼ lb) **aubergines**
5 tablespoons **olive oil**
2 **onions**, finely chopped
500 g (1 lb) **minced lamb**
300 g (10 oz) **tomatoes**,
   diced
3 pinches of **ground
   cinnamon**
pinch of **paprika**
3 **eggs**
50 ml (2 fl oz) **milk**
800 g (1½ lb) **creamy yogurt**
2 pinches of **chilli powder**
180 g (6 oz) **cooked
   partially polished rice**
120 g (4 oz) **Gruyère
   cheese**, grated
salt and **pepper**

Rinse the aubergines then slice them into thin strips using a potato-peeler.

Heat 4 tablespoons of the olive oil in a nonstick saucepan and gently cook the aubergine strips.

Heat the remaining olive oil in another saucepan and cook the onions gently until they become transparent. Add the lamb, diced tomatoes, cinnamon and paprika and season with salt and pepper. Cook over a low heat for around 10 minutes.

Whisk the eggs in a large bowl, then add the milk, yogurt and chilli powder. Mix well.

Lightly oil a gratin dish. Place the aubergines in the bottom of the dish and cover with rice. Add the meat–tomato–onion mixture. Pour over the yogurt sauce. Place in a preheated oven, 180°C (350°F), Gas Mark 4, for around 35 minutes. About 5 minutes before the end of cooking, sprinkle with grated Gruyère and return to the oven to brown. Serve immediately.

For gratin of rice with cardamom & ginger, omit the onions. Peel and grate a 1 cm (½ inch) piece of fresh root ginger. Heat 1 tablespoon of olive oil with 3 crushed cardamom seeds, then stir in the ginger and gently fry it until soft before adding the meat.

paella

paella-style

Serves **4–6**
Preparation time **15 minutes**
Cooking time **25 minutes**

2 **chicken breasts**
150 g (5 oz) **chorizo**
1 litre (1¾ pints) **chicken stock**
1 tablespoon **olive oil**
2 **garlic cloves**, finely chopped
150 g (5 oz) **green pepper**, diced
2 **tomatoes**, diced
400 g (13 oz) **short-grain rice**
200 g (7 oz) fresh shelled **baby peas**
2 pinches of **saffron threads**
pinch of **paprika**
salt and **pepper**

Dice the chicken breasts and chorizo finely.

Place the stock in a large saucepan and heat gently.

Heat the olive oil in a large paella pan, then cook the garlic until it turns golden. Add the diced pepper then the diced chicken and chorizo. Season and cook gently, turning regularly. Add the diced tomatoes and the rice. Mix well together.

Pour in the stock and the peas, bring to simmering point, then add salt followed by the saffron and paprika. Cover and cook for around 10 minutes. Lower the heat and cook for a further 10 minutes.

For seafood paella, scrub 500 g (1 lb) mussels under cold running water, discarding any that do not close when tapped. Cook the garlic, green pepper, tomatoes, short-grain rice and peas as above, replacing the chicken stock with 1 litre (1¾ pints) fish stock. About 5 minutes before the end of cooking time, add 300 g (10 oz) cubed cod or monkfish, 250 g (8 oz) raw prawns in their shells and the mussels. Shake the pan to combine and cook gently. Before serving, discard any mussels that have not opened.

paella with five vegetables

Serves **4–6**
Preparation time **25 minutes**
Cooking time **25 minutes**

2 **red peppers**
1 **aubergine**
300 g (10 oz) **green beans**
4 **artichoke hearts**, cooked
4 **garlic cloves**
1 litre (1¾ pints) **chicken stock**
1 tablespoon **olive oil**
2 **tomatoes**, diced
400 g (13 oz) **short-grain rice**
a few pinches of **ground saffron**
pinch of **paprika**
salt and **pepper**

Wash and drain the peppers, aubergine and green beans. Deseed the peppers and dice them finely. Dice the aubergine. Slice the green beans into small pieces. Chop the artichoke hearts into large dice. Peel the garlic cloves, remove the germ, then chop finely.

Place the stock in a large saucepan and heat gently.

Heat the olive oil in a large paella pan. Cook the garlic until golden then add the peppers, aubergines and green beans. Add salt and pepper and cook gently, turning regularly. Add the artichoke hearts and diced tomatoes.

Add the rice and stir well until the grains are transparent. Pour in the stock, bring to simmering point, season with salt, then add the saffron and paprika. Cover and cook for around 10 minutes then lower the heat and cook for a further 10 minutes.

For stuffed chicken escalopes, slice 4–6 chicken escalopes through the centre. Marinate for 30 minutes in the juice of 2 limes. Stuff the escalopes with five-vegetable paella, transfer to an oiled roasting tray, then place in a preheated oven, 180°C (350°F), Gas Mark 4, for 12 minutes without turning, basting regularly.

chicken & seafood paella

Serves **4**
Preparation time **25 minutes**
Cooking time **45 minutes**

150 ml (¼ pint) **olive oil**
150 g (5 oz) **chorizo**, cut into small pieces
4 **boned chicken thighs**, cut into pieces
300 g (10 oz) **squid rings**
8 **large raw prawns**
1 **red pepper**, deseeded and chopped
4 **garlic cloves**, crushed
1 **onion**, chopped
250 g (8 oz) **paella rice**
1 teaspoon **saffron threads**
450 ml (¾ pint) **chicken stock** or **fish stock**
300 g (10 oz) **fresh mussels**
100 g (3½ oz) fresh shelled **peas** or **broad beans**
salt and **pepper**
lemon or **lime wedges**, to garnish

Heat half the oil in a large paella, sauté or frying pan and gently fry the chorizo for 5 minutes, turning it in the oil. Drain to a plate. Add the chicken thighs to the pan and fry for about 5 minutes until cooked through. Drain to the plate. Cook the squid rings and prawns in the oil, turning the prawns once, until pink. Drain to the plate.

Add the red pepper, garlic and onion to the pan and fry gently for 5 minutes until softened. Stir in the rice, turning it in the oil for 1 minute. Add the saffron and stock to the pan and bring to the boil. Reduce the heat, cover with a lid or foil and cook gently for about 20 minutes until the rice is cooked through.

Scrub the mussels, scraping off any barnacles and pulling away the beards. Discard any damaged shells or any open ones that don't close when tapped gently with a knife.

Return the chorizo, chicken, squid and prawns to the pan with the peas or beans and mix thoroughly. Scatter the mussels over the top, pushing them down slightly into the rice. Cover and cook for a further 5 minutes or until the mussels have opened. Discard any shells that remain closed. Check the seasoning and serve garnished with lemon or lime wedges.

For pork & seafood paella, replace the chicken with 400 g (13 oz) lean belly pork, diced and cooked as above. Replace the squid with 8 fresh scallops with roes and the mussels with the same quantity of small clams.

surf 'n' turf paella

Serves **4–6**
Preparation time **25 minutes**
Cooking time **25 minutes**

1 litre (1¾ pints) **chicken stock**
12 **large prawns** (gambas)
2 tablespoons **olive oil**
2 **garlic cloves**, finely chopped
250 g (8 oz) **chicken breast**, diced
200 g (7 oz) **pork loin**, diced
2 **tomatoes**, diced
400 g (13 oz) **short-grain rice**
2 pinches of **ground saffron**
pinch of **paprika**
salt and **pepper**

Place the stock in a large saucepan and heat gently. Wash and dry the prawns.

Heat the olive oil in a large paella pan. Cook the garlic until it turns golden, add the prawns and fry for 2 minutes. Remove from the pan. Add the chicken and pork. Season to taste with salt and pepper. Add the diced tomatoes.

Add the rice and stir well until the grains are transparent. Add the stock and bring to simmering point. Add salt and the saffron and paprika, cover and cook for 10 minutes, then lower the heat, add the prawns and cook for a further 10 minutes.

For rabbit & butterbean paella, soak 125 g (4 oz) butterbeans overnight in plenty of cold water. Drain the beans, bring to the boil in a saucepan of fresh water, boil for 10 minutes, then simmer for 1–1½ hours until tender. Drain and set aside. Cook the recipe as above, omitting the prawns and replacing the pork loin with 200 g (7 oz) diced rabbit breast. Add the butterbeans for the last 10 minutes of cooking.

mexican rice

Serves **4**
Preparation time **10 minutes**
Cooking time **7 minutes**

2 **courgettes**
1 **red pepper**
1 tablespoon **vegetable oil**
400 g (13 oz) **cooked long-grain rice**
2–3 pinches of **chilli powder**
4 tablespoons **pine nuts**
4 tablespoons **coriander leaves**
salt and **pepper**

Wash the courgettes and red pepper and cut them into small dice.

Heat a lightly oiled nonstick pan and turn the diced vegetables in it for 5 minutes, stirring with a wooden spoon. Season.

Add the rice and chilli powder to the pan and mix well. Heat for 1–2 minutes then add the pine nuts.

Serve warm, sprinkled with coriander leaves.

For hot Mexican rice with tomatillos, add 3 diced green jalapeño chilli peppers to the pan with the vegetables. Add 200 g (7 oz) of canned tomatillos (small green tomatoes), drained, with the rice and chilli powder.

rice with olives & peppers

Serves **4–6**
Preparation time **15 minutes**
Cooking time **20 minutes**

4 **tomatoes**
3 tablespoons **olive oil**
1 **yellow pepper**, diced
1 **red pepper**, diced
4 **garlic cloves**, finely
  chopped
2 pinches of **chilli powder**
140 g (4½ oz) pitted **olives**
2 **onions**, sliced
200 g (7 oz) **long-grain rice**
350 ml (12 fl oz) **warm**
  vegetable stock
salt and **pepper**

Wash and skin the tomatoes. Dice the flesh coarsely.

Heat 2 tablespoons of the olive oil in a pan. Add the diced peppers and cook gently over a low heat until soft. Add the diced tomatoes and the chopped garlic. Season and sprinkle with 1 pinch of chilli powder. Cover and cook gently for around 15 minutes. Add the olives towards the end of cooking.

Meanwhile, heat the remaining oil in a pan, add the chopped onions and brown gently, stirring regularly. Add the rice and mix well. Pour in the warm vegetable stock. Bring to simmering point and add the other pinch of chilli powder, season and cover. Simmer for around 15 minutes.

Serve the hot rice accompanied by the vegetables.

For tacos with olive & pepper rice, spoon a little of the hot rice into ready-made taco shells. Top with a spoonful of soured cream and a spoonful of guacamole. To make a chunky guacamole, mash the flesh of 3 ripe avocados and add 1 large tomato, skinned and diced, the juice of 1 lime, 1 finely chopped small red onion, 1 finely chopped red chilli and a handful of coriander, finely chopped.

spicy rice with chicken

Serves **4**
Preparation time **10 minutes**
Cooking time **15 minutes**

1½–2 tablespoons
  sunflower oil
3–4 **garlic cloves**, finely
  chopped
3–4 **small bird's-eye
  chillies**, lightly bruised
425 g (14 oz) **skinless
  chicken breast fillets**,
  finely sliced
1 **red onion**, thinly sliced
750 g (1½ lb) **cooked Thai
  fragrant rice**, chilled
2½ tablespoons **fish sauce**
handful of **Thai sweet basil
  leaves**

Heat the oil in a wok or large frying pan.

Stir-fry the garlic and chillies over a medium heat for
1–2 minutes or until the garlic has lightly browned.
Add the chicken and onion and stir-fry for 4–5 minutes
or until the chicken is cooked.

Add the rice and fish sauce and stir-fry for another
3–4 minutes. Taste and adjust the seasoning. Add the
basil leaves and stir-fry until the basil begins to wilt.

Spoon on to 4 warm serving plates.

For rice with sweet chilli prawns, replace the chicken,
garlic and small chillies with 425 g (14 oz) raw peeled
prawns and 2–3 tablespoons of garlic-flavoured sweet
chilli sauce. Stir-fry the prawns for 2–3 minutes, add the
sweet chilli sauce and mix together. Remove to the outer
edges of the wok or pan. Add the onion, rice and fish
sauce and continue as above.

rice with saffron & dried fruit

Serves **4–6**
Preparation time **10 minutes**
Cooking time **15 minutes**

80 g (3 oz) **raisins**
80 g (3 oz) **pitted prunes**
40 g (1½ oz) **dates**
1 tablespoon **vegetable oil**
2 **onions**, chopped
200 g (7 oz) **long-grain rice**
350 ml (12 fl oz) **warm water**
pinch of **ground saffron**
40 g (1½ oz) **almonds**
salt and **pepper**

Place the raisins in a bowl and cover with warm water. Do the same with the prunes. Split the dates and remove the stones.

Heat the oil in a pan and cook the onions gently for a few moments, stirring frequently. Add the rice and blend well. Add the warm water flavoured with the saffron. Season to taste, cover and cook over a low heat for around 12–15 minutes. Add the dried fruit and almonds 5 minutes before the end of cooking. Serve warm.

For rice with chicken & apricots, wash 200 g (7 oz) dried apricots and cut each one into quarters. Place in a bowl and cover with warm water until softened. Drain the apricot pieces, saving the juice. Make the juice up to 350 ml (12 fl oz) with warm water, add the saffron, and use for cooking the rice. Add the apricots to the rice 5 minutes before the end of cooking with the almonds and 375 g (12 oz) diced cooked chicken breast.

prawn jambalaya

Serves **4**
Preparation time **15 minutes**
Cooking time **20 minutes**

180 g (6 oz) **long-grain rice**
1 tablespoon **vegetable oil**
1 **red pepper**, diced
2 **onions**, sliced
2 **garlic cloves**, finely
   chopped
1 **celery stick**, chopped
1 **sprig of thyme**, leaves only
30 **raw peeled prawns**
Tabasco sauce
salt and **pepper**
knob of **butter**, to serve

Cook the rice creole-style for 15 minutes (see page 12). Drain it and set aside to cool.

Heat the oil in a large nonstick pan. Add the pepper, onions, garlic and celery. Sprinkle with thyme. Cook for 15 minutes, stirring regularly. Season.

Stir in the prawns and a drop of Tabasco and cook for a further 5 minutes. Add the cooked rice and mix well with a fork to separate the grains.

Add a knob of butter just before serving.

For jambalaya with sausage & chicken, stir
¼ teaspoon of chilli powder, ½ tablespoon of turmeric and ½ tablespoon of Cajun seasoning into the vegetables in the pan, omitting the thyme, then add 250 g (8 oz) chicken, boned and skinned, and 175 g (6 oz) sliced chorizo. Continue cooking as above.

wild rice jambalaya

Serves **4**
Preparation time **15 minutes**
Cooking time **30 minutes**

125 g (4 oz) **wild rice**
1 teaspoon **olive oil**
50 g (2 oz) **celery**, chopped
½ **red pepper**, cored,
  deseeded and diced
½ **green** or **yellow pepper**,
  cored, deseeded and diced
1 **onion**, chopped
1 rasher **rindless lean back
  bacon**, trimmed of fat
2 **garlic cloves**, crushed
2 tablespoons **tomato purée**
1 tablespoon chopped **thyme**
125 g (4 oz) **long-grain rice**
1 **green chilli**, deseeded and
  finely chopped
½ teaspoon **cayenne pepper**
400 g (13 oz) **canned
  tomatoes**, drained
300 ml (½ pint) **chicken
  stock**
150 ml (¼ pint) **dry white
  wine**
250 g (8 oz) **raw medium
  prawns**
parsley, to garnish

Place the wild rice in a saucepan with water to cover.
Bring to the boil and boil for 5 minutes. Remove the pan
from the heat and cover tightly. Leave to steam for about
10 minutes until the grains are tender. Drain.

Heat the oil in a large nonstick frying pan. Add the
celery, peppers, onion, bacon and garlic. Cook, stirring,
for 3–4 minutes until the vegetables are soft. Stir in the
tomato purée and thyme. Cook for another 2 minutes.

Add the wild rice, long-grain rice, chilli, cayenne pepper,
tomatoes, stock and wine. Bring to the boil. Reduce the
heat and simmer for 10 minutes until the rice is tender
but still firm to the bite.

Stir in the prawns and cook, stirring occasionally, for
5 minutes, until the prawns have turned opaque. Spoon
into large warmed bowls. Scatter with coriander or parsley
and serve with crusty bread, if liked.

For chicken & prawn jambalaya, omit the wild rice and
increase the quantity of long-grain rice to 250 g (8 oz).
Soften the celery, peppers, onion and garlic as above,
omitting the bacon. Remove from the pan and heat
1 tablespoon of olive oil in the same pan. Add 200 g
(4 oz) chicken breast, cut into chunks, and fry until
golden on all sides. Return the softened vegetables to
the pan, then add the remaining ingredients up to and
including the white wine. Bring to the boil, then complete
the recipe as above.

desserts

coconut rice with cardamom

Serves **4**
Preparation time **5 minutes**
Cooking time **30 minutes**

100 g (3½ oz) **short-grain rice**
seeds from 2 **cardamom pods**
500 ml (17 fl oz) **milk**
2 tablespoons **water**
40 g (1½ oz) **grated coconut**
40 g (1½ oz) **soft brown sugar**
1 sachet **vanilla sugar**

Wash the rice in cold running water and drain well.

Grind the cardamom seeds finely, using a pestle and mortar.

Place the milk and ground cardamom in a heavy-based saucepan. Bring to boiling point then pour in the rice. Cover and cook gently for around 25 minutes.

Meanwhile, pour the water over the grated coconut. Add the brown sugar, vanilla sugar and rehydrated coconut to the saucepan of rice. Cook gently for a further 5 minutes.

Place the coconut rice in small bowls and allow to cool slightly.

Serve warm or well chilled.

For coconut rice with caramelized banana, gently heat 50 g (2 oz) caster sugar, ½ teaspoon of vanilla essence and 2 tablespoons of hot water in a pan until the sugar melts and caramelizes. Stir in 15 g (½ oz) unsalted butter then add 2 ripe but firm bananas, peeled and cut into diagonal slices, and coat them gently in the caramel. Serve the coconut rice warm, topped with slices of caramelized banana.

bananas with sticky rice

Serves **4–6**
Preparation time **10 minutes**
  + 3 hours steeping time
Cooking time **15 minutes**

100 g (3½ oz) **sticky rice**
3 **bananas**
500 ml (17 fl oz) **coconut milk**
60 g (2½ oz) **caster sugar**
½ teaspoon **vanilla extract**

Wash the rice: place it in a large bowl of water and steep for at least 3 hours. Rinse several times and drain well.

Place the rice in a saucepan, cover with water and bring to the boil. Simmer gently for around 12 minutes.

Peel the bananas and slice into rounds.

Place the coconut milk, caster sugar and vanilla extract in a large saucepan. Heat gently for 5 minutes then add the banana slices. Continue cooking for a further 10 minutes.

Leave to cool, then serve with the hot rice.

For figs with sticky rice, replace the caster sugar with 4 tablespoons of clear honey and add the finely grated rind of ½ an orange. Heat as above, then add 4 fresh or soft dried figs, cut into quarters and continue cooking for a further 5 minutes. Leave to cool, then serve with the hot rice, sprinkled with a few fresh thyme leaves.

plain rice pudding

Serves **4**
Preparation time **5 minutes**
Cooking time **30 minutes**

100 g (3½ oz) **short-grain rice**
500 ml (17 fl oz) **milk**
40 g (1½ oz) **caster sugar**
1 sachet **vanilla sugar**

Wash the rice under cold running water and drain well.

Place the milk in a heavy-based saucepan. Bring to the boil then add the rice. Cover and cook gently for around 25 minutes.

Add the caster sugar and vanilla sugar, stir well, cover and cook for a further 5 minutes.

Place the milky rice in small serving bowls and allow to cool before serving.

For Indian rice pudding, bring 500 ml (17 fl oz) milk to the boil then add 100 g (3½ oz) basmati rice, 4 lightly crushed green cardamom pods and 2 saffron threads. When the rice is nearly cooked, add 40 g (1½ oz) caster sugar, 1 tablespoon of flaked almonds and 1 tablespoon of finely chopped pistachios. Finish the cooking over a very low heat.

vanilla rice pudding

Serves **4**
Preparation time **10 minutes**
Cooking time **25 minutes**

100 g (3½ oz) **partially
  polished short-grain rice**
  or **cooked wholegrain rice**
½ **vanilla pod**
500 ml (17 fl oz) **milk**
rind of ½ an **unwaxed lemon**,
  cut in strips
50 g (2 oz) **soft brown sugar**
12 g (½ oz) **butter**, diced
2 **egg yolks**
salt

Wash the rice under cold running water and drain well. Pour it into a large saucepan of lightly salted boiling water and cook on a low heat for around 10 minutes. Drain.

Split the vanilla pod lengthwise. Place the milk and the vanilla pod in a heavy-based saucepan. Bring to simmering point then add the rice and lemon rind. Cover and cook gently for around 10 minutes.

Add the brown sugar and take the saucepan off the heat. Stir and add the diced butter. Allow to cool for a few seconds.

Whisk the egg yolks in a bowl and mix them into the milky rice. Cook gently for another 5 minutes, stirring regularly.

Remove the vanilla pod and lemon rind. Divide the rice among small bowls and allow to cool slightly before serving.

For vanilla rice pudding with orange & sultanas, replace the lemon rind with orange rind and the soft brown sugar with caster sugar. Add 75 g (3 oz) sultanas and ½ teaspoon of ground cinnamon to the milk with the rice and orange rind. Continue cooking as above.

caramel rice pudding

Serves **4**
Preparation time **5 minutes**
Cooking time **30 minutes**

100 g (3½ oz) **short-grain rice**
500 ml (17 fl oz) **milk**
25 g (1 oz) **caster sugar**
1 sachet **vanilla sugar**
2 tablespoons **liquid caramel**

Wash the rice well under cold running water and drain.

Place the milk in a heavy-based saucepan. Bring to boiling point and pour in the rice in a stream. Cover and cook gently for around 25 minutes.

Stir in the caster sugar and vanilla sugar and mix well. Cover and cook for a further 5 minutes or so.

Divide the rice among small bowls, allow to cool, then refrigerate.

Drizzle some liquid caramel over each bowl just before serving.

For rice pudding crème brûlée, make the rice pudding as above, using only 1 tablespoon of caster sugar. Divide the rice pudding between 4 individual heatproof ramekins, allow to cool, then refrigerate. An hour before serving, remove from the refrigerator and sprinkle 2 teaspoons of demerara sugar evenly over each pudding. Place under a very hot preheated grill until the sugar caramelizes. Allow to cool, then return to the refrigerator for 45 minutes before serving.

chocolate rice pudding

Serves **4**
Preparation time **5 minutes**
Cooking time **30 minutes**

100 g (3½ oz) **short-grain rice**
5 tablespoons **cocoa powder**
500 ml (17 fl oz) **milk**
1 small **cinnamon stick**
50 g (2 oz) **soft brown sugar**

Wash the rice under cold running water and drain well.

Dissolve the cocoa powder in 4 tablespoons of the milk.

Place the remaining milk, the cinnamon stick and the dissolved cocoa in a heavy-based saucepan. Bring to boiling point then pour in the rice in a stream. Cover and cook gently for around 25 minutes.

Add the brown sugar, blend well, cover and cook for a further 5 minutes. Remove the cinnamon stick.

Divide the chocolate rice pudding among small serving bowls and allow to cool slightly.

For mocha rice pudding, dissolve 4 tablespoons of cocoa powder and 2 teaspoons of instant espresso powder in 4 tablespoons of the milk and continue as above. Add the grated rind of ½ an orange with the brown sugar.

rice pudding with drunken raisins

Serves **4**
Preparation time **10 minutes**
  + 30 minutes soaking time
Cooking time **2 hours**

50 g (2 oz) **raisins**
2 tablespoons **fortified wine**
  (such as Pedro Ximénez,
  Madeira or sweet sherry)
65 g (2½ oz) **pudding rice**
25 g (1 oz) **caster sugar**
600 ml (1 pint) **milk**
25 g (1 oz) **unsalted butter**,
  diced
large pinch each of grated
  nutmeg and **cinnamon**

Put the raisins in a small saucepan with the fortified wine and warm together, or microwave the raisins and wine in a small bowl for 30 seconds on full power. Leave to soak for 30 minutes or longer if time allows.

Grease a 900 ml (1½ pint) pie dish, then put in the rice and the sugar. Spoon the soaked raisins on top, then cover with the milk. Dot with the butter and sprinkle with the spices.

Cook in a preheated oven, 150°C (300°F), Gas Mark 2, for 2 hours until the pudding is golden on top, the rice is tender and the milk thick and creamy. Spoon into bowls and serve with spoonfuls of extra-thick cream.

For traditional rice pudding, omit the raisins and fortified wine and add the rice and sugar to the greased pie dish. Pour over 450 ml (¾ pint) milk and 150 ml (¼ pint) double cream. Dot with butter as above, then sprinkle with freshly grated nutmeg. Bake, then serve with spoonfuls of strawberry jam.

chocolate risotto

Serves **4**
Preparation time **5 minutes**
Cooking time **20 minutes**

600 ml (1 pint) **milk**
25 g (1 oz) **golden caster
  sugar**
50 g (2 oz) **butter**
125 g (4 oz) **risotto rice**
50 g (2 oz) **hazelnuts**,
  toasted and chopped
50 g (2 oz) **sultanas**
125 g (4 oz) good-quality plain
  dark chocolate,
  grated, plus some to decorate
brandy (optional)

Heat the milk and golden caster sugar in a pan to
simmering point.

Melt the butter in a heavy-based pan, add the rice and
stir well to coat the grains. Add a ladleful of the hot milk
to the rice and stir well. When the rice has absorbed the
milk, add another ladleful. Continue to add milk in stages
and stir until it is all absorbed. The rice should be slightly
al dente, with a creamy sauce.

Add the hazelnuts, sultanas and chocolate and mix
quickly. Serve decorated with a little grated chocolate.
Don't overmix the chocolate as a marbled effect looks
good. For a special treat, add a splash of brandy just
before decorating and serving the risotto.

For chocolate & orange rice pudding, add the finely
grated rind of 1 orange when heating the milk and sugar.
Make the risotto as above, then stir in 2 tablespoons of
orange juice, 125 g (4 oz) grated milk chocolate and
75 g (3 oz) chopped tropical dried fruit instead of the
hazelnuts, sultanas and plain dark chocolate. Reserve a
little of the grated chocolate for decoration.

rice pudding with crystallized orange

Serves **4**
Preparation time **5 minutes**
Cooking time **30 minutes**

100 g (3½ oz) **short-grain rice**
500 ml (17 fl oz) **milk**
rind of 1 unwaxed **orange**, cut in strips
40 g (1½ oz) **crystallized orange peel**, diced
40 g (1½ oz) **caster sugar**
pinch of **salt**

Wash the rice under cold running water and drain well.

Place the milk in a heavy-based saucepan. Bring to boiling point, add the salt, rice and orange rind, cover and cook gently for around 25 minutes.

Add the diced crystallized orange peel and the caster sugar. Stir in, cover and cook for a further 5 minutes.

Remove the orange rind. Divide the rice pudding among small serving bowls and allow to cool slightly before serving.

For rice pudding with pineapple & ginger, peel ½ a small, sweet pineapple, cut it into 2 cm (¾ inch) slices and cut each slice into wedges, discarding the hard core. Roast the pineapple wedges with 50 g (2 oz) unsalted butter, 75 g (3 oz) caster sugar and 1 tablespoon of ginger syrup in a preheated oven, 200°C (400°F), Gas Mark 6, for 30 minutes, basting frequently. Meanwhile, make the rice pudding, replacing the crystallized orange peel with 1 tablespoon of finely chopped preserved ginger. Serve the rice pudding topped with the roasted pineapple.

rice with mango

Serves **4–6**
Preparation time **5 minutes**
  + 1 hour steeping time
Cooking time **12 minutes**

200 g (7 oz) **sticky rice**
2 tablespoons **soft brown sugar**
250 ml (8 fl oz) **coconut milk**
4 tablespoons **warm water**
1 **mango**, thinly sliced

Place the rice in a large basin and cover with water. Leave to steep for at least 1 hour. Rinse well and drain, then place in the centre of a clean cloth.

Heat some water in the bottom compartment of a steamer. Place the cloth containing the rice in the upper compartment. Take care to spread the rice out in an even layer. Cover and cook for around 10 minutes.

Open the cloth, wait 1 minute for the rice to cool, then place it in a shallow serving dish, fluffing it up well.

Place the brown sugar, coconut milk and warm water in a saucepan. Blend well and bring to simmering point. Remove from the heat.

Pour the coconut milk syrup over the rice. Leave to cool. Just before serving, add the sliced mango.

For fragrant rice pudding with mango, cook 200 g (7 oz) Thai jasmine rice creole-style (see page 12), adding 1 stem of fresh lemongrass, split lengthways, to the cooking water. Drain the rice and discard the lemongrass. Place 200 ml (7 fl oz) coconut cream in a saucepan with 2 tablespoons of golden caster sugar and 4 tablespoons of warm water and continue the recipe as above.

sweet saffron rice with honey peaches

Serves **4**
Preparation time **25 minutes**
  + 30 minutes steeping time
Cooking time **30 minutes**

100 g (3½ oz) **basmati rice**
500 ml (17 fl oz) **milk**
pinch of **saffron threads**
vegetable oil
40 g (1½ oz) **flaked almonds**
70 g (3 oz) **honey**
4 **peaches**
20 g (¾ oz) **butter**
pinch of **salt**

Wash the rice under cold running water, turn into a bowl and cover with water. Leave to steep for 30 minutes then drain carefully.

Heat the milk gently in a heavy-based saucepan, add the saffron threads and a pinch of salt, cover and leave to infuse for 10 minutes.

Heat a nonstick, lightly oiled pan, add the rice and cook gently for a minute. Add the almonds. Remove the saffron from the milk and stir 50 g (2 oz) of the honey into the hot milk, blend well, then pour over the rice mixture. Cover and cook over a low heat for around 20 minutes.

Meanwhile, bring a large saucepan of water to simmering point. Plunge the peaches into the water for 1 minute, then run them under cold water. Skin them, slice in four and remove the stones. Heat the remaining honey and the butter in a nonstick pan. Add the peaches and cook gently on one side for around 2 minutes, then turn them and cook for a further 3 minutes.

Fluff up the grains of rice with a fork and turn out into one or several small moulds. Unmould when ready to serve with the pan-fried peaches.

For maple-syrup rice with pecans, omit the almonds and peaches. Cook the rice as above, replacing the honey with 50 g (2 oz) maple syrup. Heat 20 g (¾ oz) maple syrup with 20 g (¾ oz) butter, add 125 g (4 oz) pecan nuts, roughly chopped, and heat gently for 2 minutes. Serve rice topped with the pecan nuts.

coconut rice with peaches

Serves **4**
Preparation time **5 minutes**
Cooking time **30 minutes**

100 g (3½ oz) **short-grain rice**
500 ml (17 fl oz) **milk**
40 g (1½ oz) **grated coconut**
50 g (2 oz) **caster sugar**
1 sachet **vanilla sugar**
4 ripe **peaches**
a little **lemon juice**

Wash the rice under cold running water and drain well.

Place the milk in a heavy-based saucepan. Bring to boiling point then pour in the rice in a stream. Cover and cook gently for around 25 minutes.

Add the grated coconut, caster sugar and vanilla sugar. Blend in well, cover and cook gently for around 5 minutes. Divide the coconut rice among small serving bowls and leave to cool, then refrigerate.

Peel and quarter the peaches. Process them to a fine purée and sprinkle with lemon juice.

Serve the chilled rice with the peach purée.

For coconut rice with raspberries, process 500 g (1 lb) fresh or thawed frozen raspberries to a purée with 2 tablespoons of caster sugar. Stir in the finely grated rind and juice of 2 limes. Serve the chilled rice with the raspberry purée.

rice pudding with spices & coconut

Serves **4**
Preparation time **15 minutes**
  + 30 minutes steeping time
Cooking time **30 minutes**

100 g (3½ oz) **basmati rice**
500 ml (17 fl oz) **milk**
1 **clove**
1 small **cinnamon stick**
50 g (2 oz) **caster sugar**
1 sachet **vanilla sugar**
50 g (2 oz) **grated coconut**

Wash the rice under cold running water, then place it in a large bowl and cover with water. Leave to steep for 30 minutes, then drain well.

Heat the milk, clove, cinnamon stick, caster sugar and vanilla sugar in a heavy-based saucepan. Bring to simmering point. Add the rice, blend well, cover and cook over a low heat for 25 minutes.

Heat a nonstick pan and add the grated coconut. Stir well until it begins to turn golden.

Remove the clove and cinnamon stick. Divide the rice among small serving bowls. Let cool, then sprinkle with the toasted coconut.

For rose & cardamom rice pudding, replace the clove and cinnamon stick with 2 teaspoons of rose water and 2 lightly crushed green cardamom pods. Replace the toasted coconut with 50 g (2 oz) lightly toasted flaked almonds.

creamed rice with orange-flower water

Serves **4**
Preparation time **5 minutes**
Cooking time **10 minutes**

6 tablespoons **white** or **brown
rice flour**
1 litre (1¾ pints) **milk**
90 g (3½ oz) **caster sugar**
2 tablespoons **orange-flower
water**
60 g (2¼ oz) chopped
pistachios

Blend the rice flour with 4 tablespoons of the milk.
Place the remaining milk and the diluted rice flour in a
heavy-based saucepan, stir well and bring to simmering
point. Cover and cook gently for around 10 minutes,
stirring regularly.

Add the caster sugar and orange-flower water, stir well
and take the pan off the heat.

Place the creamed rice in small serving bowls and leave
to cool. Sprinkle with chopped pistachios and serve at
room temperature.

For creamed rice with dried fruit compote, place
50 g (2 oz) each of chopped dried pears, apricots and
prunes in a saucepan, cover with water, bring to the boil,
then simmer for 5 minutes. Remove from the heat and
leave to steep while making the creamed rice as above.
Serve the rice topped with the dried fruit compote and
chopped pistachios.

red rice risotto & sautéed grapes

Serves **4**
Preparation time **15 minutes**
Cooking time **50–60 minutes**

75 g (3 oz) **unsalted butter**
175 g (6 oz) **Camargue red
  rice**, rinsed with cold water
  and drained
750–900 ml (1¼–1½ pints)
  milk
½ teaspoon **ground mixed
  spice**, plus a little extra
  to decorate
50 g (2 oz) **light muscovado
  sugar**
250 g (8 oz) **red seedless
  grapes**, halved
crème fraîche

Heat 50 g (2 oz) of the butter in a saucepan, add the
rice and cook gently for 2 minutes, stirring. Heat the milk
in a separate saucepan, pour about one-third over the
rice and add the spice.

Cook the rice gently for 40–50 minutes, stirring
occasionally until the rice is tender and creamy, topping
up with ladlefuls of milk as the rice swells and stirring
more frequently towards the end of the cooking time.

Remove the rice from the heat and stir in the sugar.
Heat the remaining butter in a frying pan, add the grapes
and fry for 2–3 minutes until hot. Spoon the risotto into
shallow bowls, top with spoonfuls of crème fraîche, then
spoon the grapes and a little extra spice on top. Serve
immediately.

For cherry risotto, fry 175 g (6 oz) white risotto rice
in 50 g (2 oz) butter, then cook with 600–750 ml
(1–1¼ pints) warmed milk as above, omitting the
ground spice and adding 1 teaspoon of vanilla essence
and 50 g (2 oz) dried cherries instead. Simmer gently
for 20–25 minutes until the rice is soft and creamy. Stir
in 50 g (2 oz) caster sugar. Omit the grapes and top the
risotto with spoonfuls of crème fraîche.

index

acknowledgements
Photographs by Akiko Ida. ©
shutterstock: Monkey Business
Images 2–3; mundoview 4–5;
Babajaga 9; Mates 23. Octopus
Publishing Group: David Loftus
157, 221; David Munns 144–145,
204–205; Eleanor Skan 116–117,
189; Ian Wallace 43, 59; Lis Parsons
66–67, 73, 89, 91, 93, 155, 159, 161,
165, 182–183; Stephen Conroy 6–7,
34–35, 94; Will Heap 123, 143, 219,
235; William Reavell 151, 163, 203.

Dining set on page 79, Robert le
Héros.

Styling by John Bentham.

Executive Editor: Eleanor Maxfield
Managing Editor: Clare Churly
Translation: JMS Books LLP
Art Director: Jonathan Christie
Picture Library Manager: Jennifer
Veall